The Experience

of Marriage

The

Experience

of Marriage

THE TESTIMONY OF CATHOLIC LAYMEN

EDITED BY *Michael Novak*

The Macmillan Company, New York

For Jim and Pat who preceded us

and for Richard and Patricia

who introduced us

Contents

Introduction

THIS UNUSUAL COLLECTION of essays grew out of the conviction that lay Catholics have said in public only a fraction of what they have to say about the actual experience of Catholic marriage. Private conversations are invariably much more intense, incisive, and various than public statements have been. As a result, it seemed to many that the honesty of the Catholic body was being compromised. The Church has nothing to fear from honesty, and if laymen have not spoken sooner they must themselves accept the responsibility. It is, then, as loyal sons and daughters of the Church that the contributors to this volume have written—even the non-Catholic partner, in the mixed marriage represented, speaks with good will toward the Church. This collection is a sign of responsibility, loyalty, and trust.

On no subject, of course, is honesty so difficult as that of sex. Surrounded by social and personal inhibitions, the realities of sex are not easily brought out into the open even under the best conditions. Few would deny, moreover, that American religious people in general, and American Catholics in particular, have not been blessed with or have not yet created a good environment for frankness about sex. American Catholics, as more than one contributor to this volume testifies from his own experience, seem afraid of sex, slightly guilty about it, ill at ease in discussing it.

But besides this general difficulty, it seems that although

the usual categories for the discussion of sex in American Catholic circles—control, indulgence, the "rendering of the debt," primary and secondary ends of marriage, the "use" of intercourse, and the like—might well serve the legal purposes of canon law, still they ill serve the realities of daily experience. It is not that these categories are necessarily in contradiction to daily experience; it is only that they apply to marriage from a point of view and in words unfamiliar to most married persons. In the nature of the case, marriage in canon law and marriage as it is lived do not seem to be the same. It will no doubt be useful to theologians to have before them the testimony of those who live marriage day by day, as an additional source of insight into an important part of the Catholic experience.

There is, moreover, a further motive in the presentation of these essays. This motive is the belief that an empirical method is as fruitful for theology, in those places where it borrows from philosophy, as it is for philosophy. It is no secret that at present moral theologians are obliged to borrow their conception of the "essence" of marriage from the usage of the word "essence" in the contexts of canonical jurisprudence. Surely, a decision about what constitutes the act of intercourse, the generative faculty, and the purposes of marriage will be enriched if it includes recognition of the testimony of how this act, this faculty, and these purposes are experienced by Catholics in daily life. In seeking criteria for defining the nature of the marital act, we cannot take merely a biological point of view, nor a merely legal point of view. If we study the concrete reality, perhaps we shall find that the definition of intercourse as "an act *per se* apt for generation" is a biological abstraction; and that the description "penetration by the male organ of the female vagina, and ejaculation" is a legal abstraction. Perhaps neither one will then seem sufficient as a philosophical or an empirical definition of marital intercourse. A human, not an animal, act is at stake, and it may well be fuller in its nature than previous generations of men understood. Natural law may ask fuller requirements of marital intercourse than men heretofore have recognized.

In any case, whether the experience of married couples leads theologians into such reflections or not, the public testimony of laymen will make it easier for theologians to understand the audience to whom they voice their conclusions, whatever those conclusions might be. As one contributor to this volume writes: "Those of us who love Mother Church and who are loyal to her give you the last word. But you must speak it." And all the contributors seem to insist: "Mere repetition of the tradition is not enough. Our moral dilemmas are new. Medicine, economics, new self-consciousness, higher levels of education have compounded the moral problems of married life. Help us."

The task of inviting the contributors to this volume was at first perplexing. The editor desired a group that was national in composition, of varied experience, and of different outlooks. He hoped that the contributors would be able to write adequately, for nothing is more difficult than breaking through the clichés of one's mind in order to say what one means; many persons have much deeper, and more honest, ideas than they know how to put into words. He solved these perplexities by making up a tentative list of eighteen contributors from around the country, whom he knew personally, by reputation, by letters to editors in magazines or newspapers, or by the recommendations of others. To each of these couples he sent a form letter outlining the nature of the projected volume, and asking them either to contribute or to recommend some friend who might contribute. From the beginning, the proposal of anonymity was included, so that honesty and frankness would be encouraged.

Of that original list, seven couples agreed to write, and four others volunteered the names of acquaintances who, in the end, replaced them. Out of fortuitous conversations or letters in which the subject of the projected volume arose, other contributors were added. The editor, thus, has never met many of the contributors, and barely met most of them; nor are they known to one another. This sampling is not scientific, but neither have its results been preconceived. Only the public response it receives will reveal how typical are the variety of marital experiences it presents.

In the editor's correspondence with the many contributors, and also with those who in the end could not contribute, the original conception of the volume underwent inevitable changes. The one crucial point was that the volume reflect daily experience; that point did not change. There was, besides, no attempt to structure the contributions in any particular way. With several contributors, the editor had a chance to make this point especially plain; most took it for granted. Nevertheless, it will probably be useful to repeat here the relevant portions of the original letter which set the volume in motion. The letter could have been worded more carefully, and its emphasis could have been different. Fortunately, the contributors made up for its inadequacies. In any case, readers may be grateful for a glimpse of the original conception, however modified it became.

For some time it has been obvious that discussions of the role of sexuality in Catholic marriage have suffered from too much theory and too little fact. Laymen have said in public only a fraction of what they have to say about the actual experience of Catholic marriage. If there is to be a worthy theology of marriage, surely such a theology cannot be begun until there is available an empirical base on which to build it.

To this end, [the editors of the Macmillan Company] have agreed to publish a volume of testimony from Catholic couples about "The Experience of Catholic Marriage." Might I ask you if you would like to contribute to this collection?

In order to allow a maximum of frankness, we have decided to publish the contributions anonymously, describing each author only generically: ". . . is a professor at a midwestern university; has been married 10 years; has 5 children." You might offer your own description of yourself.

Whenever possible, husband and wife should collaborate or,

preferably, contribute separate statements—we are extremely anxious that the experiences of the wives, so much neglected in this area of discussion, be given due attention.

It is essential to the success of this volume that it not be theoretical. It is not a polemic against present Church discipline. It is not an outlet for fledgling philosophies of sex or marriage. It is an attempt to *describe* the daily concrete realities of sexual life and marriage, in order to undercut the naïve and misleading theories of sexual life and marriage now so prominent in public discussions.

Some questions to which contributors might address themselves are the following: What is your dominant moral anxiety in the use of sex? Did you experience a conflict between what you had been taught in earlier sex education and the reality as you came to live it? How applicable to your experience is the concept of indulgence, or self-control? Have you practiced rhythm, and with what results? Has coordination in climax been difficult to achieve, and did the difficulty cause you moral concern? What has the use of sex taught you, from the point of view of moral growth? How have you reconciled the moral demands made upon you by your children and those made by your professional tasks? Under what conditions has the exchange of love been most beneficial to you as persons? Have you experienced difficulty in being honest with yourself and your faith? How important is the use of intercourse in your marriage? Of abstinence? etc.

Allow me to conclude with the remark that you may well write the article in an impersonal tone if direct first-person language is too uncomfortable; the articles may refer to the experiences of friends, too, but they should not generalize too widely. They are an attempt to give a largely cleric-oriented discussion a turn toward the actual experience of married people, whether or not this experience coincides with theory. The leading question is: "What has sexuality in marriage actually meant to you as persons and as Catholics?"

This letter, of course, was an attempt to break through the usual modes of thinking about sexuality, but it probably fell into the opposite vice of reading too much like a standard medical or psychological manual—there was a bit of the clinical about it. In sending out the second wave of letters, therefore, the editor was able to emphasize that the questions posed by the letter were not to be taken in any sense as a structure for the replies, but only as a means of releasing the couples to find language of their own. The following articles indicate that the contributors were quite able to pursue independent lines of inquiry. They had obviously given their vocation much thought. Only, heretofore, they had not had the opportunity to voice their views.

This volume is, therefore, happily diverse and uneven. Some contributors write with unmistakable polish; others manifest an honest but rougher style. The minds of some went in one direction, the minds of others in another. The book is no doubt the more authentic and the more rewarding for these differences. On the other hand, there are some things which the contributors did not get around to saying, and on a few matters one or another has made a factual mistake. It did not seem wise to correct the latter difficulties in the original text, not even by discreet footnotes. But in order to make the book as useful as possible to a wide audience, perhaps it would be well to note some of these matters now, at least in a general way.

In the first place, sometimes the impression is given that "nothing" is being done by Catholics, laymen or clerics, toward solving the severe problems of fertility and infertility, the growth of populations, and the rest. But the truth is that matters are moving so swiftly in the Church on these questions that almost every year brings its new "breakthrough"; so much so that it is difficult to generalize even over a five-year period. Not to mention Dr. Rock's admirable work in Boston these last many years, we must note other efforts and sources of information already in existence. Georgetown University has recently established a research institute on population questions; New York City and Buffalo give a home to important clinics; the Family Life bureaus in various dioceses—Chicago, for example —are increasingly active and effective. In Europe, such centers as Amis du Levain (1, rue de l'Abbé-Grégoire, Paris VI) and

Editions Xavier Mappus, who publish the important *Fiches documentaires du C.L.E.R.*, (11, rue Ste-Hélène, Lyons 2) make available, almost on a monthly basis, documentation and reports on developments in all phases of the question of marriage: theological, medical, psychological, sociological, educational, and bibliographical. And yet, having noted these efforts, we must admit that one of the most striking things in the discussion of marriage among American Catholics is the inadequacy of communication, the failure of sources of information. Useful and even crucial information is simply "not getting through." Nor can laymen easily shift the blame for this situation; lay responsibility is a two-edged sword. One wonders why more Catholic doctors, lawyers, businessmen, and others do not invest time and money in solving the many problems which, after all, affect them too.

In the second place, there seems to be a wider latitude about the licity of using steroids than some of the contributors to this volume recognize. Louis Dupré, for example, has noted ("Toward a Reexamination of the Catholic Position on Birth Control," *Cross Currents*, Winter, 1964) that a number of theologians approve of wives using steroids during the time of nursing the baby, on the grounds that "ideally" nature intends that period as an infertile one. Moreover, a long letter published by Father Michael O'Leary of the Archdiocese of Detroit, in a national magazine (*Jubilee*, March, 1964) and with the *nihil obstat* and *imprimatur* of the diocese, indicates the divergence of opinion among moralists on the essential morality of the antiovulants. Fr. O'Leary cautions married couples to wait prudently until other moralists have a chance to consider his views. But he argues that it cannot be shown that antiovulants are wrong *in se*, everywhere and always. And if they are not wrong in themselves, then, perhaps, not only may they be used according to the principle of double effect, in order to regulate an irregular cycle, for example, but also whenever in real marital situations the couple have a right to avoid a pregnancy and are not acting selfishly. This is not the place to evaluate his argument or to decide difficult moral issues; but it would be remiss to allow the impression to be made that moralists are not hard at work on these issues, in an ever broader context and with ever more data to assimilate.

Finally, there is the ever-lurking question of continence as a spiritual ideal in marriage, and of the "spiritualization" of married love. Many of the contributors in this collection come near to saying, but none quite say, that marital sexuality itself involves spiritual ideals. We are not taught to think this way. The emphasis is on abstinence; no one urges us toward wise, ripe sexuality, or speaks of the importance of sexuality in our Christian development. Some of the contributors voice warnings against the many modern, romantic views of sexuality, and such warnings are surely sensible.* It remains that our human sexuality is intimately connected with our emotions, attitudes, self-image, and even our conscience. Our sexuality affects the whole texture of our lives.

In this sense, of course, sexuality has a wider rather than a narrower range. It certainly does not mean merely the traditional philosophical or legal definition mentioned above. When husband and wife express their love for each other in the marriage act, they are, whether they are aware of it or not, bringing much of their whole lives to that act. They are intimately and—it might be said—dangerously affecting each other, for good or for ill. There is no way to escape such interaction. To ignore it, to act as if it were not occurring, to neglect it in one's descriptions or theories is not to make it go away. It is to cover it up.

In practice, of course, men and women express their love in the marriage act with various degrees of awareness. The act of love can be just another act. It can be merely the fulfilling of a biological or emotional need, as rhythmic as eating—though,

---

* I have tried to spell out some of these romantic views in "Marriage: The Lay Voice," *The Commonweal*, February 14, 1964.

perhaps, more surrounded with inhibitions. It can be made to seem as the great ecstatic foundation on which the rest of life is built. The human sexual act is susceptible of these and many other interpretations; it is vastly complicated. But perhaps it is at least permissible to argue that human sexuality will be made to yield up its secrets best if it is approached on its own terms. To judge sexuality in the light of abstinence is surely misleading. Human sexuality is one of those things of which Genesis says: "God saw it, and saw that it was good." But what, specifically, *is* good about human sexuality? What moral and spiritual values lie latent in it? How can it be that Christians have neglected to reflect upon sexuality and draw from it all the secrets that God has written into it?

In many languages, the radical sense of that most central of human verbs, "to know," points to the act of marriage. Is it thereby indicated that in the act of marriage we can most radically come to know ourselves and each other? It should be possible to begin listing the ways in which the act of marriage unites, binds, and educates each couple. No doubt, in practice we may derive too little nourishment for our spirits from the act of marriage. We may expect too little from it—or too much—simply because our expectations were allowed to develop in one way or in another. But whatever be the periods of continence which married couples wish to observe, and must observe, it is not upon the periods of continence but upon the periods of expressiveness that they must begin to reflect if they would discover the ideals and values special to married life. The attempt to "spiritualize" their love may, moreover, be a serious misunderstanding, just as it would be misleading to attempt to spiritualize the Church. It may be true that in heaven there will be no marrying nor giving in marriage, but neither will there be external church, hierarchy, or even faith and hope. If we are to accept, to respect, and also to love the human condition, it seems that we must learn to appreciate human sexuality just as we appreciate the external church.

This volume, in short, represents early, sometimes faltering steps toward a just estimation of the experience of marriage. Each of the contributors, in his or her fashion, and with his or her aims in mind, has tried to take marital sexuality on its own terms, as it has entered into his or her experience. Many of the contributors found much brush to clear away before they could begin to speak clearly, and all of them had too few words for their task. Each could no doubt say still more if he or she were asked, and under face-to-face questioning each might elaborate or modify his or her account.

The editor hopes that in the coming years much more of this face-to-face questioning will take place among the Catholic people, and between small groups of them and their pastors. And he also hopes that to many couples in America, about to wed, newly wed, or long wed, this volume will bring a sense of companionship with many other couples. He hopes that it will be greeted with an expression of sober recognition: "No, our marriage is not quite like any of those in the book; and yet— we see our faces in them as in a mirror."

CHAPTER ONE

Permanent Continence

Mr. and Mrs. A have been married six years and have four children. Both parents attended Catholic schools through college. Mr. A currently teaches in an Eastern college.

Mr. A writes first:

Not long ago my wife and I celebrated our sixth wedding anniversary. Those six years had not yet brought us to the age of thirty, but they had brought us four children, for whom we are very thankful, and a growing burden of financial, medical, and psychological difficulties which have made any further expansion in our numbers an improvident risk. Our situation can hardly be an exceptional one among young Catholic couples. So, too, it is probably not extraordinary that we have also discovered during these six years that the rhythm method of birth regulation, by which we had hoped to space out the intervals between births, is clearly ineffective in our case, even with all the elaborate help of temperature readings, mathematical calculations, and medical consultation. Hence, we have taken the only other alternative now open to Catholic married people who see birth regulation as a moral imperative: sustained continence.

Moralists sometimes call this choice "heroic"—as they do its alternative, the acceptance of whatever future progeny may come despite foreseeable problems and complications. If we are not mistaken, Catholic writers have in recent years become less sanguine about this second sort of "heroism." But not much at all has been written about the first, perhaps with reason: from our limited experience we can see how discouraging such "heroism" is in actual life. If we are not quite certain that it ought to be called "heroic," we can understand why doctors and psychiatrists call it dangerous, and why some people call it absurd. We have found it no less absurd than the practice of rhythm, and somewhat less detrimental to our personal growth in married love. But these are ambiguous statements, and demand explanation.

Six years of marriage are not a terribly long time, but within that period we have been man and wife trying to grow in Christian married love—conjugal love, as some writers put it —within three kinds of contexts. The first context, at the start of our life together, was one of learning to love as man and wife, of integrating a new and wonderful physical experience into our personal relationship. This context provided its own particular problems, but was not complicated by a need to avoid pregnancy. The second context was established after the birth of our second child, when it became evident that for reasons of physical and mental equilibrium it would be better to avoid another immediate pregnancy. This can be called the "rhythm context." After this method had proved unreliable and we had our next two children, it was clear that the context would have to change again—this time to one of sustained continence. Apart from the ordinary difficulties of a rapidly growing family, each of these contexts brought new demands and new challenges; each has had profound effects on our experience and understanding of love and sex; each has influenced in one way or another our growth as Christian persons.

The puritan moralist, who is apparently not a stranger in

the Catholic tradition, might see in this speedy succession of contexts an outline of the way of Christian perfection for the married layman: sexual activity in marriage leading to procreation; the burdens of procreation leading in turn to a necessary "transcendence" of sexual activity; man and wife finally sustained by a "more perfect" love that has no need of sexual expression. Fortunately or unfortunately (depending on how closely you advocate this angelistic pattern), the reality is quite otherwise. At least that is what our own experience indicates so far. The calculated continence of living with rhythm, and the anticonjugal continence of living with "heroism" have both in fact killed something in our common life which was able, at its best, to provide a tone of harmony and joy which could support us through the inevitable tensions and trials of family life, which could actually *help* us to behave like Christians. Now, with that tone lost, we find it more difficult than ever to maintain a visible spirit of Christian love, to be patient and kind toward each other and toward our children. Fidelity to the obligations of Catholicism in one direction has erected new obstacles to living a Catholic family life of charity.

But, one may ask, what *real* connection is there between Christian charity and the sexual love of man and wife? What kind of love can we have if it can be influenced so strongly by the lack of physical intercourse? I would suggest two things here. First, this question assumes that there is a dichotomy between body and spirit. It arises from that angelistic view which considers the sexual "part" of man as somehow basically unworthy of, and always a threat to, man's higher nature. From this point of view, to think of intercourse simply in terms of the physical is all too easy—and to my mind pernicious. For if the experience of Christian marriage reveals anything to a couple, it is that whenever sexual activity is reduced to the simply physical, it becomes radically inhuman, impersonal, and a violation of love. For a husband and wife in love with each other, there can be no better expression of their mutual self-surrender

than sexual intercourse, when each brings the totality of himself
as a person to the other. The "two in one flesh" of Genesis, it
seems, points to this same recognition.

The second point I would stress is that the married life,
vivified by sexual love, does somehow provide a strength and
a harmony which encourages Christian attitudes and behavior:
generosity, patience, tolerance, dedication, and above all,
charity. There is a joy in marital sexual union which overflows
into the other activities of life. The psychologist may understand this as the result of a measure of human fulfillment. The
theologian may see here a verification of the sacramental nature
of Christian marriage. They may in fact be talking about the
same thing. Somehow, hard as it may be to explain, the experience of this strength and joy is bound up with sexual union in
married life. When sexual union is missing, love is not
destroyed, but it is deprived of its most adequate symbol and
support. If I may dare to make the comparison that best il-
lustrates the point to me, marital life without sexual union is
like Christianity without the Mass, or like the Mass without
Communion.

I do not presume to suggest that such an awareness of the
positive relationship between married love and the Christian
life results automatically from the experience of sex in Christian
marriage. Sexual life is as prone to distortion and imperfection
as Christianity itself, and it takes a constant effort to keep
things in balance and order, and in the direction of maturity.
The ego or the Old Man, as St. Paul would put it, is always
trying to reestablish control over the human spirit. But since
Christ is truly with us, and since He is with married people in
a special sacramental way, the Christian has all the more reason
to see in married sexual love *his* way to wholeness in Christ.
Sexual love in marriage does not seem to be simply a concession,
or a duty, or a temporary reward, which in the last analysis it
is best to transcend.

If I look back at the orientation toward sex which was given me (largely by indirection) in my Catholic education through high school, I cannot find much that would support a positive view of sexuality. I can remember the blushing embarrassment of the priest in high school who introduced our religion class to the encyclical on Christian marriage. From the instruction given in retreats and in the confessional, the sexual element in man emerged as basically a danger and a temptation, the devil's chief means of destroying the integrity of youth. Not until college did I discover clearly the more positive things that Catholicism has to say about sex in human life. My intellectual orientation became more balanced and mature, but it was not easy for my emotional attitudes to keep pace; the past burdens of personal moral anxiety could not be set down so easily. Hence it is perhaps surprising that the experience of love and marriage should have been so overwhelmingly decisive in reorienting my deepest attitudes and insights. The predominant tensions and difficulties had disappeared by the start of my married life. There were different ones later on, but the reality of married life with my wife was more than enough to reveal the truth of the more positive things we had learned and talked about with regard to marriage.

The first context of our married life, then, got off to a good start. The tenderness that had been developed in our earlier relationship found its natural growth and ultimate expression in the complete act of love. We learned how the union, self-giving, and fulfillment of that act brought us to an awareness of each other and of ourselves quite unlike anything we had ever experienced or even imagined before. I understood for the first time really what richness is involved in the biblical metaphor of *knowing* one's wife. I cannot explain it, but it is there, and each mutual act of love recreates it, renews it, and never fails to astound me with its wonder and its mystery. Yet sexual union is not all glory and ecstasy. Like all neophytes in marriage, we discovered in the sexual side of our relationship surprises, humor, and difficulties.

It took us some time, for instance, to learn how to coordinate our climaxes. The phrase, I know, has a terribly clinical tone about it, but the fact behind it is important on the inter-personal level. Sexual union that is consciously sought for as self-gratification (and there are times when such desires present themselves) is automatically a failure—no one ought to be surprised about that. It may bring pleasure, but it does so at the expense of another person, and hence represents a failure of personal love. Sexual union is successful as a very special encounter between persons when each person is consciously directed to fulfilling the needs and desires of the other; and this conscious aim finds its most adequate symbol in the coordina-tion of climax.

Since this is not always easy to achieve, there is a tendency on the husband's part, for example, to feel some sense of per-sonal failure if he cannot bring his wife to her climax at the proper moment; he feels he has failed the person, not the "task," which is a different thing entirely. The problem reveals something very significant about human sexual activity—that it is essentially ordered to the good of the other. When the good of the other is not wholly achieved, or when it is not wholly intended, one is aware of a defect; in the latter case I would judge the defect a moral one. In sexual union, to place the self before the other is to mar the meaning of sexuality which is suggested by experience itself. The essential joy of sexual union reveals itself only in mutual donation, never in self-satisfaction. It is a joy of personal union, where each makes it possible for the other to express the strength of his or her desire at the same time as he or she helps to meet the needs of the other in love.

Because sexual experience reveals itself in this way, part of the process of maturing in love involves a growing sensitivity to the needs of the other person, not only in the act of love itself, but also in all the other dimensions of married life. But once again, the expression of one's sensitivity to the other's needs finds its most precious and conjugal form in sexual activity. From this focus seems to spring the broader joy and harmony that pervade a happy life together. On the practical everyday level, there are many things to learn about the other, especially because husband and wife each bear a different kind of sexual psychology.

From the very beginning the man learns to practice restraint and self-control, so that his wife will be able to find fulfillment in each sexual encounter. There will be times when he will sense in his wife a lack of desire for sexual activity, even though he may feel very eager himself. If he does not respect the mutual nature of sexual union, he injures her, distorts the meaning of the act, and indeed injures himself. This is so very basic in the psychology of married love that I am continually amazed at writers who seem to think that married couples who are not practicing restraint in connection with rhythm, for example, are giving themselves over to unbridled sensual indulgence. Sexual love by its very nature demands self-control and the capacity for self-sacrifice; otherwise it is not love. No couple, and certainly no Christian couple, will face the challenge of restraint for the first time, only when they need to practice rhythm or continence. Restraint is a part of every love relationship worthy of the name. And it is *always* a challenge, especially for the husband, whose sexual drives and needs are usually more consciously persistent than those of his wife.

Thus we discover at the very core of married union a constant call for charity, an inevitable demand to fuse *eros* with *agape*. At times the only way to answer that call will be to avoid sexual union; at others, union itself will be the proper response. Husband and wife learn to recognize the differences in their patterns of sexual response, and to respect those differences, out of love. Each becomes more sensitive to the needs of the other, knowing ever more clearly when the other's needs may be greater than his own. By "needs" I do not mean simply physical needs, but personal ones: the interlocking physical, psychological, and spiritual needs that arise from the complex and unique relationship between two personalities living in close intimacy, a relationship that involves many different kinds of emotional ups and downs, many different kinds of responses and reactions to day-by-day events and moods. Because sexual love involves so much more than physical release, because it brings with it a close spiritual unity, strength, and comfort between persons, it becomes an appropriate response to many of the unpredictable and varied tensions generated by family life and its problems. From this perspective, it is not so much an escape as it is a mutually sustaining gift which husband and wife have the power to bestow upon each other.

As a young family grows, and the demands of caring for children become ever greater, the day-to-day problems, difficulties, and sacrifices grow and increase as well. The challenges of maintaining a Christian atmosphere of peace and harmony in the family multiply rapidly and surprisingly, as any mother of several young children can testify. The assaults on individual serenity and balance increase steadily in strength and frequency. Now, more than ever before, the sense of mutual encouragement and support, mutual tenderness, humor, and play that pervades personal sexual union becomes a crucial help. Although the occasions for mutual sexual activity inevitably diminish with the increased strains and burdens of maintaining a growing household, they become more highly cherished and more deeply needed than ever before.

But now the progression of married life brings with it some disturbing paradoxes. When the trials of the family situation are such that the birth of further children must be postponed, or in some cases avoided, the Catholic couple must turn to periodic or sustained continence. If they have been directing their sexual life in charity, the problem of individual restraint will not be a new one. But the very burdens and strains of family life which transform sexual union into a less frequent and more crucial personal experience of mutual dedication and support now either rule out sexual union entirely or narrow its scope still more.

Those who try rhythm turn to the aid of calendar calculations, daily temperature readings, the plotting and interpretation of graphs, hoping thereby to arrive at some approximate knowledge of when they may allow their mutual love and affection to overflow into its fullest and most complete expression, and when they may not. The uncalculated and spontaneous pattern of their life in love must be altered to suit this scheme. The invitation to sexual love, once established by the happy confluence of mutual endearment, mutual vitality, and mutual responsiveness, no longer comes from the unchartable interior relationships of man and wife; it comes from the external calculations.

Inevitably, the conduct of personal interaction must also change: when the chart says "no," the couple must act out a common role of sexual indifference and personal distance, which for a man and wife deeply in love is indeed a forced and inappropriate role. When the chart says "yes," it is not simply a question of becoming normal again for a week or two. Whether we like to admit it or not, something new enters into the relationship, something which might be called the "Mardi Gras complex": the semiconscious pressure to exploit the possibilities of the safe period as much as possible. Probably for the first time in their married experience, husband and wife begin to sense a compulsion toward sexual union even when the mutual interior disposition may be lacking. This aspect of rhythm, more than anything else in marriage, seems to be the strongest force in converting sexual union into a kind of mechanical ritual. Together with the aspect of forced indifference, this compulsiveness reveals the rhythm method as one that involves a basic danger to the interior, personal, and mutual nature of human sexual intercourse. The personal harmony between two human beings, elevated by *caritas,* is now in greatest danger of being subordinated to an external "harmony" between the couple's sexual life and the chart.

The periods of forced indifference tend to destroy a certain tone of married life which is psychologically very important. It is the tone set at the start of married life, already fore-shadowed in courtship: the tone of playfulness, of mutual sharing in a very private and joyous game. It has something to do with the fun of sexual attraction and pursuit, with the mutual and integral enjoyment of each other to the fullest extent. This fun and this joy are never sheerly physical; they involve, once again, the whole person. The moves of the game are not always sexual, but they are always capable of leading spontaneously and naturally into sexual play and union. A young husband and wife do not have to calculate or plan the fun they enjoy in each other's company; it is *there*, it endears them to each other, it enhances their union, it is good for their morale (and, by the way, for the morale of their children), it is good for keeping each other from neglect. The trouble comes when rhythm demands that this tone be switched off for two weeks or more each month of their life together.

An outsider may wonder whether it is necessary to "switch off" this sense of play. Cannot love, mutual interest, and sup-port be expressed in ways that are independent of sex? Of course they can. But not very adequately for the balanced life of a *married couple* wholly given to each other. It is the unique quality of human sexual love between man and wife to be "always there," a total personal gift that can be both desired and granted independently of temporary biological fertility. Sexual union, which the psychology of man and wife ex-periences as a kind of ultimate and most significant expression of their belonging and giving to each other, is the most special sign of *married* love. Tokens of affection and love between man and wife, though not directly sexual themselves, tend to build toward a self-giving that is sexual. It is impossible for a husband to love his wife simply as a "sister" or a "friend" or even "another Christian"—the bond of intimacy between them is specifically sexual or conjugal, and tends naturally and spontaneously to express itself in this way. Since it is an expression of this sort, intercourse itself loses something of greatest importance when it must be planned or calculated. And for the same reason, a man and wife will only increase their frustration if they try to keep alive their sense of play and courtship at times when sexual union is ruled out by the chart.

In what has been said so far about the disturbing elements in the practice of rhythm, I have purposely ignored the most disturbing element of all: its all too common inefficacy. I have done this because I think it important to stress that even with a "perfected rhythm system"—should such be possible—a married couple faces problems that may threaten the quality and harmony of their love relationship, problems that are of crucial importance to the psychology of love, and perhaps of equal importance to the morality of love.

The psychological difficulties that beset the couple using rhythm are magnified immeasurably by the inevitable fact that the method is uncertain. Uncertainty as to whether the so-called safe period really has been safe generates constant tension and anxiety. Whether conception has in fact been avoided in any particular month of the wife's menstrual cycle is never known until menstruation occurs, and then a new cycle of anxiety and doubt begins. This can be particularly detrimental to the wife, whose fear of possible pregnancy can effectively eliminate her ability to desire and enjoy sexual union. The uncertainty of the system transforms human intercourse from an expression of love to a threat to the well-being of the family. And when a man and wife are forced to interpret things in this way, they do more damage to themselves and to their union by risking intercourse than by eliminating it altogether.

Thus arises the distressing dilemma facing so many married Catholics today: either they risk the good of the family and the health of the wife by making another pregnancy possible (and such an alternative does not carry with it a very meaningful or joyous kind of sexual union), or they risk the psychological damage and frustration of a wedded life without sexual union. Either way, something very good and enriching and conjugal must be sacrificed; either way, one will find new obstructions to growth in charity. The pity of it is that in each case what must be sacrificed is something intimately bound up with the whole nature of marriage as "two in one flesh," as St. Paul's mystery of mutual Christian dedication. The dilemma involves more than the Cross, the challenge of suffering which every Christian must face. God knows how many such challenges are already present in married lives uncomplicated by this dilemma. The dilemma involves, in some way, a basic absurdity.

Experience brings out the absurdity in full force. In the one case, the husband's loving embrace of his wife is as much as to say, "I love you, and with your consent I am willing to risk your health and the well-being of our family." In the other case, it says, "I love you, but I should not be holding you this way because it may prove dangerous to your well-being or to our moral life." We are left either with a love that is not wholly love or with a marriage that is not wholly marriage.

Catholic marriages are not the only marriages that can fall prey to boredom and indifference, that can fall apart from the inside because husband and wife have lost their sense of union, their sense of mutual dedication and self-donation. They are not the only marriages that can substitute for such union another kind of relationship: a family complex in which the father loses himself in his work and the mother loses herself in her children, while both draw farther apart from each other. But Catholic marriages that preclude sexual union leave themselves more open to such developments. Some may see in such a transformation the required order of things. But we cannot. If the dedication to our children does not proceed from our dedication to each other, something is wrong, something is missing. So it is with love, with patience, with our sense of humor. If these do not have their source and focus in the personal bond between the two of us, they are somehow defective. Is it only youthful idealism and romanticism that sees things this way? The psychologists and psychiatrists say no. The moralists are not certain. But our experience is firm in its lesson that the demands of periodic and sustained continence encourage the transformation of husband and wife into estranged functionaries.

And so our life has become a battle to stay together in a personal way despite the contrary battle we must wage to stay apart in a physical way. Because our past relationship has been built upon an integral unity in which the physical and personal have been interdependent, the present polarity strikes us as both confusing and depressing. Man and wife, we force ourselves to live as though we were unwed. We sleep apart, we avoid each other's presence, we stifle the words and gestures of tenderness that once could blossom into sexual love. We are aware that some Catholic writers have advocated for such cases as our own the exchange of physical intimacies short of intercourse, and even intercourse short of orgasm, but such alternatives only intensify and aggravate the tensions and burdens of living together in such an unnatural situation. Sexual activity, instead of being directed by charity, becomes directed in such cases by the weird and distasteful principle of "just so far and no more." *What* one is doing becomes the center of psychological focus, and the *person* is lost in the process. The power of will displaces the sense of humanity; sex is reduced once again to a mechanism. It is far better to avoid it than to bring it to this.

The sexual factor in our marriage, then, for a short time so positive and rich a force, has now become in our third context of married life a negative force, a threat, and a danger. What "two in one flesh" meant for us once is now an abstraction and a memory. In its place we have something like a "permanent occasion of sin." A sense of wholeness, balance, harmony, and even fun is gone from our lives, and we pray to learn a way to revive it in other forms. We pray, too, that the tension and nervous anxiety with which we are now living, and which breaks out in cruel ways sometimes toward each other and toward our children, will not permanently injure our personal union and the inner life of our children.

Without prayer and the sacraments, of course, without the hope that what we are doing is indeed God's will, such a situation would be simply intolerable. Even so, I would not be honest if I implied that I can face the necessities of the present situation and the prospect of the future with anything like full serenity and conviction. To feel one's life being converted in such a way that increasing psychological tension and moral anxiety become its persistent marks, is no encouraging experience. To admit this is perhaps to admit that I lack the proper Christian spirit. This may well be true. Nonetheless, I would join then with all imperfect Christians in asking the disturbing question that perhaps has never been asked with the force it deserves: Is this what it means to live the vocation of Christian marriage?

His wife's postscript:

For six years I have been married to a very kind and understanding man whom I love completely. These have been unquestionably the happiest years of my life. This is not to say that there have not been difficult times and even bad times. But the grace of the sacrament and the wonder of children, the strength and beauty of both physical and spiritual love transcend the difficulties. There is a sense of fullness and completeness in married life which somehow makes it possible not only to bear the burdens of the life but to grow and build upon them.

Of course, one of the outstanding problems in most Catholic marriages stems from the Church's position on family planning. For us this is currently a very real problem. The rhythm method simply will not work for us. We have already had two babies while practicing the strictest form of rhythm. We were married five years and one month when our fourth child was born, and the fourth pregnancy was particularly difficult because of serious diseases I had contracted during the pregnancy. Our doctor, a non-Catholic, advised against further babies. He recommended the anovulant pill (if my conscience would allow it), but since that was out of the question he gave me more temperature charts. He made it perfectly clear that he thought there was little hope in the rhythm method and that he could see no sense to it at all. The only alternative for us has been total abstinence, which we have now practiced for more than a year.

It is unbelievably difficult, and I am doubtful that we will be able to keep it up when I think of the number of childbearing years we have left—possibly twenty! The worst part of living this way from my point of view is that it kills much of the joy that should be implicit in a marital relationship. For example, I know that physically this is intensely more difficult for my husband than it is for me. I feel guilty when we kiss or show any more than the simplest and most rudimentary signs of affection. I no longer flirt. I simply must keep a physical distance. This is extremely difficult when a woman is naturally affectionate and very much in love with her husband. However, I feel that this is the only way this "system" will work. If I do not limit and curtail my natural affections there is danger of grave sin or more babies. It sounds hopeless and very bleak, and I suppose in a way it is.

But strangely enough and quite paradoxically there is still a very real happiness in my married life, for which I am terribly grateful. It is not a complete life and when lived this way never can be. It is a life of sacrifice and hard work and grace. It is a life lived in good faith and hope and trust in the goodness and love of Christ and of each other. And that trust in each other and in Him somehow makes it possible to live and grow in a love that does not become depleted although at times it is desolate; does not despair although at times questions; does not become forlorn and lonely but at times must desire and be denied; does not shrivel and die out but sometimes cries for hope; and always exalts in the wonder of living together in Him and for Him and with Him.

CHAPTER TWO

"A Harsh and Terrible Thing"

Mr. and Mrs. B have been married eighteen years and have ten children. Mr. B has held many jobs and is now working overseas.

The testimony of Mrs. B:

Twenty years ago when I was studying sociology we spent many hours and words worrying about the population pyramid, which was supposed to have a broad base of babies and a few centenarians at the peak. Instead it tapered in with a low birthrate from the depression years, and we could recite the effects: conservative foreign and domestic policies because the men in power were getting older, bankruptcy of baby-carriage companies unless they switched to manufacture of wheelchairs, closing down of schools, and so forth.

When my senior class voted that they wanted to have an average of 6.6 babies, we thought they would be doing a real service to the country, and when I married, I believed that welcoming babies as they happened to come was the best part of a good marriage—biologically, psychologically, and sociologically.

If it had not been for the sudden exaggerated extension of the base of the pyramid after the war, and all the dire predictions in print about its effect on world food supply and living conditions, I would still think that was true.

There were some bad moments. When we had two babies and I discovered that I was pregnant again just as my husband had to go into a hospital with a relapse of his old tuberculosis, and when the new baby turned out to be twins, so that we had four children (the eldest only two years old), and no job, I spent several nights weeping on the edge of despair. But like so many of the people in Maisie Ward's *Be Not Solicitous,* we discovered that a baby is born with more than a loaf of bread under its arm.

A good, interesting job offer came from a man who had never met my husband but had read his articles, and it kept us in "reasonable and frugal comfort" for twelve years. Every time the landlord hinted that perhaps we were outgrowing our house, or the trolley fares became a burden, an unexpected piece of income enabled us to move to a larger home, to acquire a car, or in some way to fill the need.

We were happy, healthy, and well adjusted, and we wrote columns and gave lectures advising young married couples to stop fretting about birth control, to relax and leave the planning in God's hands.

We had no television and seldom went to the movies. Like poor people all over the world, we found love-making an exciting and inexpensive recreation. What could be more beautiful, when "the earth moves," as Hemingway said, and your conscience and your appetites pull in the same direction. Nothing is more satisfying, body and soul, than giving yourself to the one you love, and each time the act is different, so you are never sure how it will go, and never bored.

If there were friends and relatives who disapproved, we were quick to notice the flaws in their marriages: the neuroses, the alcoholism, the resentments that came from trying to fight nature.

Now we are still leading a rich, busy and, I hope, useful life, but I no longer feel that we can have babies with a clear conscience. My "dominant moral anxiety in the use of sex" is that if we produce more children we may be laying on the straw that will break the population camel's back in twenty years, and burdening our children with a real survival problem.

So we have ten, and presently we are able to support them, thank God. But is it fair to the young married couples who are entitled to have a family? Is it fair to the poor Latin Americans and Indians and Chinese who can barely find room to sleep in a makeshift shack, or a bowl of rice to eat? In the beginning, God told us to increase and multiply, and we had a duty to continue the race and people the world, but now is not the duty in the other direction? To insure survival of the human race in decent human conditions must we not refrain from adding to the mass?

Every pregnancy now brings a real feeling of guilt that we are pursuing our own pleasure without regard for the good of the whole of society.

Is there any way for us to continue to show our love for each other through sexual intercourse without burdening the bursting world? For us, within the limits of natural law as taught by the Church, almost none.

Because of my double ovulations in one month, the rhythm system is almost without value. It is possible to calculate the time of one ovulation with reference to the menstrual pattern, but the second seems to fall with utter caprice. We have conceived a child on the day before the menstrual period should have begun, and one six days from the beginning of the period.

The only time that we can have intercourse with any degree of certainty that there will not be a baby is during the first five days from the beginning of menstruation, even though my periods are regular and we are into middle age.

It may be that the pattern which has been forced upon us will help to make us truly mature. Freud said it would be a great advance when love-making was governed by rational decision rather than by animal instinct, but I miss the old spontaneity. However, this way each occasion is something very special, something to plan for, with more attention to scenery and costumes.

What has the use of sex taught me from the point of view of moral growth? That it is necessary to decide which is the greater good in a particular case, and then to do what must be done to achieve it. That it is possible to rearrange sexual habits, or to abstain altogether for a time, without any serious danger of aberrations. That if one is in a period when abstention is required, curbing consumption of alcohol makes it easier.

As for achieving coordination in climax, I think this is more of a worry for my husband than myself. Not having succumbed to what Mary McCarthy calls "the tyranny of the orgasm," I can be happy with a little extra petting if I don't make the complete fireworks' display every time. It's distressing if my husband feels in any way inadequate, but heaven knows he has enough proof of his prowess, and a few kisses will effectively smother any complaints from me.

Did I experience a conflict between what I had been taught in earlier sex education and the reality as I came to live it? Not really. The priest who prepared us for marriage gave us that excellent little pamphlet "Happiness in Marriage: An Ethico-Medical Interpretation," and if, as I have heard, its distribution has been suppressed in some dioceses, it should be resumed. It gave clear, true, inspiring directions for the uses of sex in marriage, far superior to the dozens of other books and leaflets I went through when we were giving talks on the subject.

Possibly there are good recent publications we haven't seen, but most of the old stuff was awful. At college there was a marriage course for seniors which I couldn't take because some of us had to get the newspaper to press at the hour each week when the classes were held. Every Wednesday night we would rush back to our friends and roommates and inquire whether the lecturer had come to the sex part yet, but he never did. The final week one bold student rose and asked if he intended to say anything about sex, but was told to ask her mother. There's more to marriage than sex—patience and charity are important ingredients—but to go through a semester course without mentioning sex seems unrealistic, at best.

I hope that the old confusion between ignorance and innocence in Catholic circles has been somewhat relieved by the popular pre-Cana conferences, improved literature, and the changing attitude of instructors in Catholic schools. Having been out of the country we are not in the current of contemporary American Catholic thought, but the articles and lectures which reach us are of the "put that birth control right out of your mind" school, with no mention of restraint for the good of society, and no merit allowed to the satisfaction of emotional needs unless children are the outcome.

Under what conditions has the exchange of love been most beneficial to us as persons? Emphatically it has been when we wanted to have a baby and knew that conception was likely. Superlatives are inadequate to describe the exhilaration and the feeling of fulfillment.

How important is the use of intercourse in our marriage? At this stage of middle age it keeps me feeling like a woman— important, desired, but dependent, instead of like a plant manager or the vice-president of some big corporation—running a family this size. Without it I would become a frightful shrew, with so much "pick up those pyjamas!" "Who spilled the Jell-O in the freezer?" "Why don't you call when you're going to be two hours late?" "You certainly cannot go if your Latin isn't finished!" "Eighty-nine cents a pound!" There's nothing like a little love-making to make it all worthwhile.

How important is abstinence? If there is clear mutual agreement that it is necessary, and the end a noble one, then it can be uplifting and even unifying. If I have doubts about my husband's conviction, it can be a source of guilt.

To sum up: I have thoroughly enjoyed the whole business of begetting, bearing, and rearing, and if someone could convince me that it would be the best thing for the world, I would be happy to have ten more.

Mr. B adds:

As everybody enjoys a good clean fight between husband and wife, I will start off by taking exception to two points that my wife has made.

One, she says that she worries because "if we produce more children we may be laying on the straw that will break the population camel's back in twenty years, and burdening our children with a real survival problem."

I don't worry about this. I worry about the population explosion, if that term can be properly and accurately used. I worry about improving agricultural production to feed the world's hungry children. I worry about developing underdeveloped countries. I worry about distribution of income. But I don't worry about the possibility that one or two children of mine might be the straw that breaks the camel's back.

I just can't begin to have the information to justify a sensible worry on that subject. There are too many clearcut moral problems involved in trying to be a good husband, father, man for me to worry about without devising new ones based on such problematical suppositions. Particularly when the moral supposition runs so directly counter to everything the Church has been telling us for so many years.

The Church has been saying, loud and clear, "Have as many children as you and your wife can afford to have." Actually, it hasn't always been so clear because the Church, or certain representatives thereof, have sometimes fudged the meaning of "afford." But I take it that perfectly respectable theological opinion has it that "afford" should be understood as not only financial but also physical and even psychological means. Since we have had ten children, and three miscarriages, in less than eighteen years and the baby is not yet fourteen months old, I am not disputing my wife's claim that that is enough for the time being. I think there are good reasons for this position without leaning on a theory that there are too many children in the world.

If that were true, then everybody should worry, including the parents with only two or three children.

Neither do I worry about "burdening our children with a real survival problem." That is too much like the parents who refuse to have children because it's such an awful, awful world and how can you bring yourself to condemn the poor little things to live, or die, in such an awful, awful world? I don't buy that. I think it's a wonderful world, that the gift of life is a tremendous blessing for any child, that even if life becomes awful, heaven remains to make it wonderful again, and that I must start with the supposition that God will provide for my children as He has provided for me.

And yet I don't think I would take the position that "young married couples (should) stop fretting about birth control, (should) relax and leave the planning in God's hands."

Let's go back over the personal history. As has been noted, we have had ten children. And yet I think that only three were intended at the time. So much for the *oohs* and *ahs* of nice old Catholic ladies who tell us how marvelous we are to have had so many, as if this had been a perfectly free act of will.

We tried the rhythm, but it didn't work, because of the double ovulations of my wife. Also we took some chances when we knew it was risky. Conception became sometimes a matter of desire outweighing fear. I think, looking back, that this was always by mutual consent. In any case there were enough

people to suggest afterward, in varying degrees of obvious-
ness, that you had been a beast imposing your lust upon your
poor suffering spouse.

At any rate the children came and we worried about being
able to afford them—financially, physically, psychologically.
Maybe we would have done better with them if they had been
better spaced. Maybe one or more of them suffer from some
grievous flaw that could have been avoided if we had had
fewer of them.

I can only testify from my own observation of them and our
feelings about them, and from what other people say about
them. Trying of course to extract the polite malarkey from what
seems to be an honest statement of opinion.

The consensus seems to be that they are pretty good kids,
healthy, smart, and doing well in school. Pretty good schools
too. Well fed, well clothed, well housed. We would be heart-
broken if we had to part with any one of them. All our worries
seem to have been unfounded. God did provide. Until the last
few years we were in debt a good deal, so maybe in all honesty
it should be said that our creditors provided too, and maybe
this was unfair. But mostly they were the phone company and
the oil company waiting an extra month or two, and I can't
really feel too bad about that.

I think it is accurate to say that our worries were mostly
unfounded, that every baby *is* born with a loaf of bread under
its arm, that God *does* provide.

Even so, we did use the rhythm and sometimes it worked.
And we did not have as many children as we might have, and
probably that was a good thing. So I am not going to say that
nobody should fret about birth control. I think it is beyond
dispute that some people are having more children than they
can begin to take care of and raise as decent human beings.

The most I can bring myself to say is this: From our own
experience, it seems that most people worry more than they
should about having too many children and that it is better
to lean in the direction of having what you think is too many

rather than too few. With us this worked out marvelously well. I thank God with all my heart for how marvelously well it worked out.

So I will worry about whether my wife has the physical and psychological strength to have more children. It is no longer necessary to worry about the financial resources, but I would worry less about that anyway. I will not worry about whether there are too many kids in the world already, at least not as affecting my own willingness to have more. Nor will I worry about whether my kids can support themselves in an over-populated world, at least—again—not as affecting my own willingness to have more, although it is only right and proper to worry about both these matters from the standpoint of doing everything that I can do to change the conditions of modern life so that every man willing and able to work can afford to have as many children as he wants.

Before I start to worry about limiting my own family for such global, demographic reasons I think it will be necessary for somebody like the Pope or an ecumenical council to tell me so. It is just too sensational a departure from everything they have been telling me up to date.

Now for the other thing with which I disagreed slightly. Actually, it is only a question of emphasis. My wife said that she found it was possible "to abstain altogether for a time without any serious danger of aberrations." For her this is certainly true. And for me it is also true, but there is a difference between possibility and probability. In other words, even where there is no abstinence there is always the serious danger of sin, if only from adulterous thoughts. And the longer the *enforced* abstinence—that is, enforced by fear of conception—then the greater becomes the danger of sin, whether in the direction of adultery or in the direction of treading too close to the line of onanism or false orgasm.

So I fret about birth control for several reasons. I would like to know when we are going to conceive so that every conception might indeed be a free act of will, a free and meaningful act of cooperation with God's creation, and not an accident. Secondly, I fret about it because I would like to be able to make love to my wife more frequently—complete and perfect love, that is—not simply because this would make it more easy to be chaste in my relations with her and with other women, but also because it would contribute to making our life together more beautiful, more nearly perfect.

For these reasons, and because so many people in the world are so clearly in the position where they cannot afford to have more children, I am conscious of a certain amount of resentment that the Church is not doing more to promote a safer, better, and more easily accessible method of using the rhythm. I understand that the Archdiocese of Buffalo has a clinic where the rhythm method, and how to use it effectively, is taught by Catholic doctors to any married woman who wants to take advantage of this service. Why doesn't every Catholic diocese have such a clinic? It almost reminds one of the bit in the epistle of St. James: "Here is a brother, here is a sister, going naked, left without the means to secure their daily food; if one says to them, Go in peace, warm yourselves and take your fill, without providing for their bodily needs, of what use is it?"

If the priest sits in the confessional, or stands in the pulpit, and tells the suffering faithful that they must use only the rhythm method of birth control, and then does nothing to help them find out how to use that method, of what use is it? Small wonder that so many of them, from being faithful, become empty of faith and are lost to the Church.

Also, I cannot help but believe that if the Church were really to put the full force of its weight behind it, enough money and enough interest could quickly be raised to promote research that would soon come up with a cheap, simple way of determining when a woman is fertile and when she is sterile, so that the rhythm method would be far more often a safe and sure way and not, as some wag put it, a kind of Vatican roulette.

I cannot bring myself to question the Church's teaching on

birth control. Almost instinctively, almost intuitively, I feel that the Church is right. It is almost as if my very flesh shrinks from the idea of employing any kind of mechanical device or pill to frustrate conception, to interfere with the natural performance of the act of love. Actually, there are two things here, two separate shrinkings. One is a shrinking from meddling with the internal, natural biology of the female, say, by the use of a pill to change the natural fertility of the woman to sterility. The other shrinking, which also has an aesthetic quality, is the shrinking from using some kind of device to prevent the sperm from meeting the ovum. It seems to me to violate the fitness of things, and with me personally this is enough to say, without expanding on more involved statements of natural law.

So I do not question the teaching. But I do question the sincerity, and the courage, and the conviction of some of those who teach, because they seem to be so reluctant to do anything to implement their teaching and make it possible for the faithful to accept what is, after all, a hard saying.

What else? The editor has asked us to comment on such questions as, "Has coordination in climax been difficult to achieve, and did the difficulty cause you moral concern?" The answer to the first part of the question would have to be "yes," especially when intercourse is limited to two or three times a month, as it has had to be for extended periods in our case. It causes moral concern when I feel that I have been too selfish, too impatient, and that this is perhaps responsible for the failure to achieve climax together. There is no question that the act falls short when perfect mutuality is not present, and it bothers me if there is any reason to believe that I am at fault.

I am not going to fall into the trap of disparaging sexual love, physical love. Nor would I dare to suggest that the complete act of love does not have spiritual aspects that raise it above, sometimes far above, the merely physical. Nor would I for a moment question the importance of sexual satisfaction and mutual fulfillment, or the shattering havoc that lack of these can leave behind in any union of two normal human beings.

But sometimes I think that the old fogies have a point when they maintain, usually in miserable prose, that the modern, or Freudian, world puts too much emphasis on the sexual part of married love. I have been trying to think back over the years and recall the times and the moments that contained the brightest and the deepest pleasure. I think that most of them have contained a relatively small sexual element. Of course many of them involved the children together with my wife, what you might call the joys of family love. And perhaps it is fair to point out, as my wife just reminded me, that without sex there can be no children.

What seems now to have been most characteristic of those moments, however, was their intellectual or spiritual quality. Sometimes it was the joy of laughter, which seemed suddenly to fuse the whole family into a unity of humor. Sometimes it was the gladness that came when you saw a son or daughter do something truly unselfish. Sometimes it was simply the quietness and peace and friendliness that descended, as if from God, upon the family circle and put an end, for a short sweet time, to all the wars and rumors of wars that ordinarily sweep back and forth and through the house.

I get the impression that some writers are trying to sell the doctrine that given a few more mutual orgasms, properly spaced, and any rocky marriage can flourish like the green bay tree. Was it Dostoevsky who wrote that "love in practice is a harsh and terrible thing, unlike love in dreams"? The harsh and terrible thing about married love is the struggle to overcome your own selfishness, to give up the insatiable desire to be one up at all times, one up with the wife, one up with the kids, to relinquish the romantic dream that everybody should be catering at all times to your own personal pleasure, to turn the look of the eye and the bend of the will around, from one-self to the others.

It is from soil broken up by this hard, sharp plow that the flowers most surely bloom.

CHAPTER THREE

After
Twenty Years

Mr. and Mrs. C live in Canada, where they have been raising a family of seven children. Both are college graduates, and Mr. C, now in the advertising business, once taught in a college.

Mrs. C writes:

Perhaps I can best express a wife's viewpoint of the role of sexuality in our marriage, and some of the problems linked with this role, by attempting a sort of odyssey of our experience of the conjugal relationship during the past twenty years. I can describe my reactions to the varying circumstances of our marriage; I can explain how my reactions seem to have affected my husband. But since a human relationship is never a static thing, but is a shifting interplay of action and reaction between two human partners, I cannot claim that my observations of our experience have general application to other couples. I do know from conversations with friends that *many* of our experiences are common to a great number of married couples.

To the facts you know about us from the heading of this article, I wish to add several other important ones. From the days of our love and courtship right through to our present middle age, J. and I have been somewhat idealistic and duty-oriented people. Before marriage, we looked forward to married life and to family life as a sacramental way of life. Coming as we both did from families of seven and eight children, we hoped for and expected to rear a large family of our own. And God has blessed us with the energy and the opportunities to attempt to rear our children to a sacramental view of life. In fact, we would find a life outside the sacramental framework unthinkable and impossible.

With the urgency of young love in wartime, we were married in 1943, just eight weeks before J. went overseas for two years. This honeymoon interlude was a happy time because we were together; and a painful one, as most couples will appreciate, because eight weeks is too short a time to learn to live together in peace and harmony. But upon J.'s return in 1945, we had two years of this learning process before the advent of the family.

To imagine these early months or years of marriage as a kind of carnal feast is a far cry from the truth. True, we were young and eager for this bodily experience of each other, which to us was important as the ultimate unifying force in the life we were making together. But the union of two in one flesh is not achieved in one such experience. Indeed, carnal knowledge of each other is gained slowly and painfully, amidst the normal hazards of the human condition like weariness and tension. And consideration and concern for each other's moods and needs must be learned at the same time.

Our oldest child was born, amidst rejoicing, four and one-half years after our wedding. With a miscarriage in between, our second child arrived exactly two years later. Only at this time, after nearly five years of normal married life, did it seem to me that our sexual relationship was capable of reaching a balanced and happy adjustment satisfying the needs of both of us. But this second baby, afflicted with a congenital heart defect, required an unusual amount of care—as much as eight to ten hours a day for feeding problems—and for the first time I experienced fear of pregnancy. But pregnant I was, when the baby was four months old. The next five years passed with three more children interspersed with two miscarriages. And there were our futile attempts to use the rhythm. But what chance was there to develop a rhythm chart of any kind when for four years I did not have one menstrual period, as confinement led to nursing, followed by a new pregnancy?

So far, these are only the facts. Obviously, during these years of family increase we had a sexual relationship. But what was it like? As my fear of pregnancy grew, and as I found myself bone-weary with caring for my young children, I was less and less able to respond to gestures of love and affection from my husband. Feeling that the whole burden of restraining desire was on my shoulders, I soon reached a point where I experienced none myself, and I even resented and shrugged off ordinary everyday signs of affection. My husband appeared in my eyes and in his own as an unreasonable beast with physical needs which, according to my marriage vows, I had a duty to meet. After all, grudgingly or willingly, I had to "render the debt" as the moral theology books say, and help him save his soul, though there were many times when I felt as though I might lose my own. And so I was passive and dutiful and frigid, enduring his love with no response. Where was the two-in-one-flesh relationship that should draw us together in a warm and tender union, and enable us to face the problems of providing for and educating our rapidly growing family? It seemed lost forever under a pile of conflicting emotions—resentment, bitterness, weariness, and at times, almost despair. Even our attempts at the rhythm were not wholehearted; for we had been educated, in marriage courses, to the notion that "rhythm is permitted only because of lack of faith and hardness of heart." Somehow it was second best. And during this period of five years, confessional advice went something like this: "Well, perhaps it's not God's will that your wife have a rest this year. After all, your needs are her first duty."

Still the picture was not uniformly dark. After all, pregnancy substituted a certainty for a fear and a worry! And occasionally, during pregnancy, though my shape was not the most conducive to sexual union, I managed to overcome my usual lack of interest and reassure myself *and* my husband that I was still capable of desiring him, of expressing my love for him through the joy of our conjugal relationship.

But our conjugal life was not one of peace, joy, and tenderness. Of course, it is possible, like Pollyanna, to draw good and gladness from any situation. And we did this too. We enjoyed our children and our friends. We had our close family life and our jokes. But in addition to fighting to provide for and educate our children we were fighting our own sexuality, the habit of union that should have helped us to fight life's struggle together. Instead, our sexuality loomed large in our thoughts and feelings as a source of inner conflict; for me, it seemed a part of my marriage to be feared, resented, and denied.

Four years ago, under circumstances nearly fatal to me, I lost my eighth baby. For a variety of medical reasons the doctor strongly urged no more pregnancies. And housing, income, and educational considerations all led us to the conclusion that we are carrying our maximum load as a family. Since losing that baby, then, we have been living a life of heroic continence or, to use the common phrase, living most of the month as brother and sister. But we are not "brother and sister"; we are man and wife, sharing a bedroom in a crowded and busy household. Recently we have taken off our Pollyanna spectacles and tried to analyze frankly the effects on us of living this kind of life. We have resolutely repressed every gesture of affection toward each other—touch, embrace, or kiss. Our kisses of greeting and good-bye morning and night—at least to keep up some appearance of affection before the children—have become mere perfunctory pecks. Even our manner of speaking to each other seems to be more brusque and impatient. We are more critical of each other—more like college roommates, tolerating each other's shortcomings, than like a husband and wife whose acceptance of each other's faults is infused with tenderness and love. We are like two friends who are used to each other through long habit.

As I watch my husband struggle alone to deny his naturally warm and affectionate ways, I yearn to show him my own love and appreciation. And yet I dare not. We have been deliberately shutting ourselves off from each other, turning our thoughts and feelings for each other inward upon ourselves. If we were perfect, if we did not suffer the effects of original sin, we might practice "controlled tenderness," to use a phrase current in clerical advice to married couples with these problems. But we know that with living, breathing, human beings, male and female, "controlled tenderness" is not practical, because either it leads to a conclusion we dare not risk, or it becomes an occasion of "sin." It is a gloriously idealistic notion, virtually impossible of practical application.

Psychologists and social workers report frequently that the absence of love and affection, and the denial of physical signs of affection, have damaging effects on developing child personalities. Because we are men, and not pure spirits, we know through our senses. And our conviction of the love of another person needs the constant reassurance of sensory (not sensual) signs of affection. We are wondering about the long-range effects of abjuring these signs in a marriage relationship—and are learning about those effects from experience.

During the past four years I have often asked myself: What is conjugal love? Is it just a habit of living together that two people have developed, for the practical reasons of providing for and rearing children? What happened to the desire for unity we had during courtship and our early years together? What of the promises we made that we would each place the other first, and never let our children come between us and break in upon our union? Has our marriage union no value to us as human beings? Is it only a convenience to ensure the survival and education of the race? By the time I have reached the menopause, will our *willed* separation be so habitual, so complete that we no longer have any need to be together? Will we be just two friends living together?

These are some of the questions we are asking ourselves at this critical period of our lives. As I have observed non-Catholic friends of mine, living good and useful lives, having their families, and yet maintaining their own close and tender union without the stress, the worry, the resentment, the preoccupation with sin that have surrounded our conjugal relationship, I have had the wistful conviction that a dimension has been missing from our marriage relationship. The fear of pregnancy, the sheer physical drain of annual pregnancies, the burden of caring for numerous small children, the constant weariness and exhaustion took me away from my husband and made me resent the very reason for our marriage. Both J. and I love our children, and are proud of them. It has never been a question of not wanting them once they arrived. But the main problem is the effect of the kind of life we have been forced to lead in our marriage relationship. And this problem, we are convinced, *we* must have the courage to look at, to admit, to face, as devout, even zealous Catholics, attempting in all earnestness to live a sacramental life with our family in today's world, with all its stresses and tensions.

Mr. C adds:

Over twenty years ago, M. and I decided to marry primarily because we loved each other and not primarily because we wished to enjoy each other's body, or to procreate. Not that we disdained each other physically, or were reluctant to reproduce! But our response to each other was a recognition that, together, we could live happier and better lives than we could apart. Our marriage began, therefore, as a dedication of each to the other's good, but with considerable ignorance of the conditions under which that dedication would have to be maintained and developed.

The earlier years of our marriage spanned most of my army service, followed by several years of undergraduate and postgraduate study as I prepared myself for what I thought would be my life's work. During this time our first three children were born, two of them abroad. Our second child was born with congenital heart disease, and she required hours and hours of careful daily care. The physical toll on my wife was severe. Nonetheless, the patience and the fortitude M. exhibited then has never ceased to amaze me—certainly, my insight into her worth was markedly deepened.

The consequence was, however, a decision that for some time the need to defer more children was imperative. We tried, therefore, to practice rhythm. We did not consult any priest about this decision, though at the time it was fashionable to do so. Our opinion was that God had given us minds and virtues of our own and that using these, we could see no other logical course of action. However, it turned out that my wife's cycle was nothing if not wobbly! Despite our keeping careful records, several pregnancies followed. The final one was almost totally disastrous, its termination in the eighth month resulting in the baby's death; my wife had a shockingly close call.

We were forced as a result to make some drastic revisions in our lives. We tossed out all the charts and other bookkeeping paraphernalia that are needed to make the rhythm system work. We weren't really sorry to see them go—calendar love, like calendar art, held no attraction for us. Even less attractive has been the alternative: conjugal relations that coincide with menstruation. This is a situation that finds the wife physically disinterested and the husband esthetically repelled. To use it as the only remaining resort for couples who wish to have some kind of complete conjugal life is what I describe as "the service station approach" to married love. Gone is all spontaneity, gone is the possibility of responding freely and joyfully to the impulse to express physically a union on all levels that you both have worked so hard and faithfully, with much mutual sacrifice and consideration, to establish. Alcohol, of course, can make the situation a little more bearable —it can take the edge off our "being serviced" feeling!

Is there no other alternative to this "service station" solution? I have to agree that there are other alternatives, alternatives that have been courageously accepted by many couples both in the past and in the present. But I don't think that just because other solutions exist, they are necessarily desirable.

I am reminded of the time a very close friend of mine, a priest who teaches theology in a seminary, became most eloquent in describing for my wife and me the joys and glories of heroic continence among married couples who needed to prevent further children. He painted for us what seemed to him the kind of life that would be a veritable earthly paradise. To us, it sounded like a nightmare, his vision had such an eerie lack of connection with real life. The plain fact of the matter was that he had no *real* idea of what goes on, at a variety of levels, in the lived, day-to-day relationship of a husband and wife. For him, love without passion is a way of life. For him, friendship without tenderness tactilely expressed is a condition of his chastity. For him, concern for, without complete involvement with, another person is necessary to his being minister to many. Yet, none of these things is normally and naturally true for husbands and wives.

For a husband and wife to practice continence successfully, they must take certain practical steps. As a start, out with the double bed, that solid symbol of conjugal unity and fidelity!

Separate beds help to interrupt that physical contiguity that tends to bloom so joyfully into complete physical union. But it is not only in bed that the sense of touch must be curbed. Where previously you exchanged caresses and kisses here and there throughout the day, now you must learn to restrain every natural movement of affection. If you are determined and persistent, you can in a few months learn to be "just friends." You can teach yourself no longer to be really involved with this "other" whom you have once loved body and soul, with body and soul. You can train yourself no longer to see her as "desirable," so that she is no longer a threat to your continent virtue, no longer a real physical value in your life, as a full-time wife would be. You will, of course, still have a companion of sorts, someone with whom you can safely chat, but who will embarrass you occasionally because you find her standing naked in your bedroom, or because she bursts in upon you while you're in the bath! Nonetheless, heroic purpose can overcome even this, and in time you can surely succeed in rendering your union completely sterile.

A chorus rises in the background. I am certain that I can hear many pastors rushing on wings of thunder to assure me that *they* know many couples to whom the picture I have painted above does not apply. And I am equally sure that there are couples who sincerely believe that they actually live their lives happily in such splendid and anguished isolation. I believe, too, that many of them, if questioned, would assure us that they are living the good, the happy life. However, among *my* many Catholic married friends I cannot remember hearing any such joyous hymn of praise. On the contrary, their pelvic anxiety is of such magnitude that there seems little or no room left to consider the other good things of life, let alone to thoroughly enjoy them.

When we speak to confessors, for example, they tell us that problems about sex and marriage so beset them that there is little opportunity to begin the very important business of helping their penitents develop a sturdy interior life, a life wherein conversation with God becomes a norm rather than an exception. The sad fact is that the life of the pelvis becomes an apparently insuperable obstacle to the life of prayer. The situation becomes even more poignant when you observe Protestant friends of good will living devout and joyous lives, their consciences untrammeled by the kind of sexual sludge that swamps so many Catholic marriages.

How tired we become with the many sermons and pamphlets that tax us with our "carnality!" It would appear that many confessors and moral theologians are aware only of the derelictions they hear in the confessional and thereby develop the impression that these are the real substance of the sexual relationship. It is my impression that it is the derelictions that find their way into the confessional, not the manifold beauties and joys that constitute the conjugal relationships which have no need to submit themselves to the keys of the Sacrament of Penance. It is my experience, too, that what I have come to regard as unnatural restraints on a joyful, free, and spontaneous relationship are responsible for many of the derelictions that so torture the Catholic married conscience.

The home I was born into and grew up in could only be described as a good Catholic home. Both my father and mother were unusually devout and faithful, and all of their eight children grew up in an atmosphere of faith and steady devotion to the life of Holy Mother Church. Nonetheless, the attitude toward sex was puritanical, and there was almost a Manichean disgust for the body and its operations. I left home having received no instruction about the purpose, significance, or beauty of the sexual relationship as it is expressed in marriage. This left me with a heavy burden to carry into marriage: how was I to be a good Christian husband and yet not be beastly? Later conversations with my mother made me aware that for her the sexual relationship was a burden, an act through which she served the race and contributed to her husband's purity, but which had for her no personal significance except suffering. This was the way, in her belief, in which she humbled her pride and worked out her salvation. To associate this act with a joyful means of grace and a greater growth of mutuality with her husband was inconceivable. The only help she received through the confessional was that she should submit with faith, that such a lot was God's Will for her. Fortunately, her faith was such that she did endure and persevere. But the price she and my father paid in terms of marital tensions was something that for years was visited upon us all. Only after my own marriage did I realize the source of those tensions and, consequently, understand much of the psychological upset and unrest that made many of our childhood days strained and unhappy.

Despite the fact that my mother very often confused intellectual development with intellectual pride, I decided when I left home to provide myself with the background necessary to understand the real meaning and place of sex in married life. Philosophical, psychological, and theological studies helped me to develop a habit of analysis which I brought to my own experience of marriage. As a result, I have over the years come to ask myself some pertinent questions.

Admitting that the flesh, especially in the early years, is very sweet, nonetheless I have found it very true that the sexual relationship is not simply a "carnal" act. It is rather the expression of the deepest urge to seek a complete union with one's marriage partner. This striving for unity is so profound, so overwhelmingly simple, that even to try to describe it is almost to deface it, to vitiate it. It is an experience that takes place at all levels of your being, and through its power gives you some idea of how God loves you and wants you to love Him. It is an experience that is personally, mutually rewarding. You become aware, as it were, of the profound intrinsic worth of that ineffable other with whom you share your whole vital being. You are literally transported into the deepest awareness of the other's essential being. And you are enriched and strengthened beyond anything you ever dreamed of, and you think, "How good God is to give us this intimation of Himself, of His love for us." And you know that you are truly one flesh and that nothing will ever part you and that your mutual dedication will be everlasting.

But isn't this too perfect? Well, were our St. Teresas and our St. Johns always in ecstasy? Yet, who would question their fidelity? Certainly, we have our lapses when the lesser elements of our nature intrude themselves, and we have to work to keep them subservient to the total relationship. This is the human condition. But what I am trying to say is that quite apart from the procreative function, the conjugal act has a personal significance that in the minds and hearts of married couples takes precedence over all other aspects. We know that it is neither prudent nor desirable that we produce *all* the children that it is physically possible to produce. We also know that we must honestly face up to our duties in this area and perform them. But our own experience teaches us that the conjugal act is not just something that is permissible because we are married and are having children. We know that it is of fundamental importance to developing our own personal relationship, to increasing that mutuality that we find is a very real analogy of Divine love.

In this context, therefore, I am forced to say that we find the views of moral theologians who speak of "heroic continence," of "controlled tenderness," sadly lacking in any sense of the reality of the actual situation. And we strongly think that many of the cherished views embodied in the Church's marriage legislation have been developed without any real awareness of precisely what the conjugal act contributes to a marriage. For my own part, as I read those sections in the texts on moral and pastoral theology which deal with marriage, I feel depressed. I know that abuses and perversions exist, but these are not the basis of a good Christian marriage. But I am equally depressed by the fact that the normal exercise of sex in marriage seems to be viewed by celibate canonists as immersed in carnality.

Not that we don't know how the natural sweetness of the flesh at times pushes its demands! But from experience, we know that Catholic couples sincerely striving to live the sacramental life find their union in the flesh a deeply ennobling and redeeming act. And we resent the attempt to make us think that there should be long periods of our lives when we are to be deprived of the unifying power and comfort of this union. Oftentimes, too, we despair that those celibate men who legislate for us will ever have any real awareness of or insight into the meaning of the conjugal act. Surely, we can hope for a day when our state of life is realistically recognized as, under Providence, best for us. And surely, too, we can hope for a day when celibate theologians will cease offering for our emulation virtues that properly belong to their own state. Perhaps, by then we will have married lay theologians collaborating in the preparation of new texts on the theology of marriage. Certainly, the Spirit can breathe where He will, and my steady prayer is that He breathes soon in this sorely neglected area.

CHAPTER FOUR

Rhythm

Mr. and Mrs. D have been married almost six years and have two children. Mr. D is teaching and studying for a degree in an Eastern state.

Mrs. D wrote out their joint statement:

When we were married my husband was about to enter graduate school. This meant that we would have to try to postpone starting our family for two or three years so that I could work to support us while he was in school. Practicing rhythm for that length of time did not seem like such a hardship. We felt that it was certainly preferable to postponing our life together any longer; we were twenty-four years old and had been engaged for three and one-half years. Surely during our long engagement we had had ample time to find in ourselves and each other the control, consideration, and sensitivity needed for such a "special state" of marriage.

Now it is five and one-half years and three rhythm pregnancies later. My husband is doing his best to finish his perpetually interrupted studies while supporting a wife and two children and living and working in very difficult circumstances.

We feel that there are things we have come to know about rhythm's effectiveness and effects that badly need to be said in something more than private conversation. We are continually distressed at the pathetically naïve or cruelly simplist manner in which the dynamics of rhythm in marriage are discussed in Catholic publications. This criticism ought in fact to be extended to the whole topic of marital intimacy in Catholic writing. Rhythm's effects would be better described if the nature of conjugal love were more fully discussed and understood.

The insights which seem to be lacking are those gained from personal experience and the sensitivity bred by it, which help us understand the experiences of friends and relatives. We hope these few comments will be a small start in helping others understand.

We started by using the basal metabolism record in conjunction with a record of menstrual cycles. That resulted in the first pregnancy. With a new baby the temperature record became much less practical to keep and much less accurate as an indicator of ovulation. So we tried the glucose test along with a much more conservative estimate of the probable safe period, altogether about nine or ten days out of each month. That worked for one year and three months. After the second baby it was clear that drastic measures were necessary for a while; so we confined intercourse to the last four days just before menstruation. In spite of this I found myself expecting a third baby, and we were so appalled in view of our situation at the time that we could only feel relief when the pregnancy ended in a miscarriage. What a terrible way to feel about a child who at a later time would have been welcomed with joy. So for now (and probably for the next year and a half), with considerable trepidation we have intercourse about once every three months. We are a normal, healthy married couple not yet thirty years old.

Further, we are living under conditions of unusually long work-hours, with insufficient sleep and very little relaxation, in unhealthily crowded living space, and with all the discomforts, worries, and inconveniences of a very frugal income. And in these circumstances we are constrained to live in a state of physical estrangement along with whatever additional disengagement is necessary to maintain it. We understand and so can accept for ourselves, at least, the myriad effects all these factors have on our relationship and on life at our house. It is not so easy to accept what we see it doing to our children. They should be living in a larger, drier, less draughty apartment. Their parents should spend much more time with them and be considerably less tense and overtired when they do. We know these things and many more, and cannot do anything about them.

We have obvious reason to be unhappy about rhythm's efficiency or lack thereof, but we are quite as disturbed about the effect that its practice has on marriage even when the couple are successful in planning their family through its use. Both problems are closely tied together and so must be discussed that way.

If a woman ovulated on an absolutely predictable day (and never more than once) in each menstrual cycle, so that each month a couple needed to abstain from sexual relations only on the day of ovulation, plus one day after and two days before, there would be relatively little problem in practicing rhythm. Four days of restricted intimacy would hardly present much complication to the relationship of man and wife. A couple could still be demonstratively affectionate with little serious problem of keeping themselves under control for such a short time. But even that rare creature, the woman who menstruates every twenty-eight days, can never be sure when some physical or emotional factor is going to postpone ovulation, precipitate an earlier one, or even cause an extra ovulation to occur in the same menstrual cycle. Consequently she must plan on a fertile period of eight or nine days, rather than four, to allow for a somewhat early or late ovulation. A woman with less regular cycles must calculate on her fertile period starting earlier and ending later. Methods of detecting ovulation can help her tell when her fertile period is indeed over, so that the couple need not unnecessarily abstain long past an early ovulation. But they cannot predict a late ovulation, so as to prevent the couple's waiting two weeks for it in unnecessary continence.

Moreover, the methods for detecting ovulation cannot always be relied upon to do even that. The presence of glucose in vaginal secretions at the time of ovulation can be detected and charted. Unfortunately many women have glucose present in those body fluids at all times, and in spite of the suggested techniques for dealing with it, for them the glucose test is quite crude and approximate.

The several doctors we have spoken with seem to feel the temperature method is more reliable. But its use has definite limitations, as we have learned. Upon awakening each morning, always at the same time and before rising, talking, moving around, or doing anything else which would slightly raise or lower her temperature, the woman takes her temperature orally with a specially sensitive thermometer marked off in tenths of degrees. A record of the temperatures is kept for the month. When the temperature rises three- or four-tenths of a degree and has stayed up for three or four days, it can be presumed that ovulation took place on the day the temperature rose. Awakening earlier will render a lower temperature, as will getting to sleep later than usual. Waking up later than usual, moving around before taking the temperature, or getting up during the later part of the night for any reason (a bottle, a change of diapers, a child's bad dream) will cause the temperature to be higher than it otherwise would be. And of course any illness, however minor, is likely to affect the temperature by at least a few tenths of a degree—all that is necessary to render the temperature reading something less than useful.

In addition to the fact that any illness makes it difficult to tell when ovulation has occurred, such illnesses or any strong psychological impact can cause ovulation to occur early, occur later, or make an extra ovulation occur during the same menstrual cycle. Thus if the wife gets a sore throat, not only her ovulation pattern is affected, but her temperature as well so that it is not possible to tell just what has happened when.

Therefore, the single girl who avoids crowds and germs can fairly well plot the course of her fertile and nonfertile periods. The married woman without small children who experiences no strong emotions and has unusually good health can do the same; frigidity is something of an asset in practicing rhythm. (Certainly, in this instance the Puritan idea that an unwanted baby is retribution for the wife's actually enjoying relations with her husband has some validity!) However, the wife who already has several young children, and is thus most in need of not becoming pregnant again for a while, stands the least chance of being successful in delaying the next baby through the use of rhythm—for several reasons. Her sleep is disturbed and irregular because she must get up at odd hours during the night for the children and again at whatever time the children awake in the morning. This makes a chart of her temperature useless. Further, fatigue and disturbed sleep make her more vulnerable to illness, and she is exposed to more germs than other adults because she is constantly around small children who have frequent minor sicknesses. These illnesses throw off her ovulation pattern and affect her temperature so that it is not possible to tell with reliable accuracy when ovulation did occur. Life with young children frequently has its hectic moments, and emotional turmoil can further change the time of ovulation. Of course, when the youngest child has gotten past the stage of incessant sicknesses and waking in the night, rhythm becomes fairly workable again. But since this is the time when the mother is back on her feet, it is also about the reasonable time to have the next baby. One can only conclude that rhythm is most practicable when it isn't needed and least practicable when it is.

A particularly complicated period in any marriage is the time just following the birth of a baby. Pregnancy and childbirth completely disrupt a woman's ovulation pattern. The pattern of her cycles before the birth of a baby is no indicator of what it will be afterward. A year's record of menstrual cycles is needed to determine what the new pattern is. However most doctors, feeling that such a long period of continence for young couples is impractical, will recommend that they proceed cautiously after keeping records for three months. This means twelve weeks after the six weeks of "flowing" which follow delivery, which was preceded by four weeks of continence: altogether twenty-two weeks, or five and one-half months. "Proceeding cautiously" usually means having relations only during a five- or six-day period each month between the time when it is fairly certain that ovulation has occurred and the time when menstruation begins.

An additional complication is added when the mother hopes to feed her baby the natural way, since rhythm cannot be practiced while nursing. When the new Catholic mother tells her Catholic obstetrician that she would like to nurse her baby, she will be gently asked whether she and her husband are prepared to accept the possibility of a new pregnancy now (which as an obstetrician he cannot recommend but as a Catholic he often feels he cannot discourage) or whether they intend to postpone having intercourse until three months after she stops nursing the baby. (The length of nursing time is usually about six months.) It is true that three-fourths of the women who nurse do not ovulate during the first three months of nursing and half of them do not ovulate during the entire period of nursing. The problem is that although a woman ovulates less frequently than usual while nursing, it will be in an unpredictable pattern which makes the practice of rhythm impossible. And for all its limitations, rhythm is still considerably more reliable as a means of postponing the next pregnancy than is lactation.

At the other end of the couple's fertile life is the second period, when rhythm is badly needed and is useless. When the couple are in their forties, the husband sees not so far ahead the time when he must retire and when his capacity to support and educate a family will be drastically reduced. Both partners have waning physical health and strength, and coping with young children has become far more difficult. However, the wife is going through menopause and consequently her ovulation pattern is completely irregular and totally unpredictable. A pregnancy at this time, in terms of health, family economy, and psychological strain could be exceedingly difficult. The only sure (and permissible) solution to the quandary is to suspend the exercise of conjugal rights for the one to three years necessary for the wife's change of life to be completed. Adjustment to the psychological effects of diminished femininity are hardly helped by total continence.

Under the best of circumstances, that is, when there are no special physiological complications and no extraordinary psychological strains, rhythm introduces a most undesirable artificiality and abnormality into marital intimacy. The unmarried are apt to think of conjugal love in terms of something which one chooses to indulge in or not, an attitude that married people find ludicrous. Since sex for the celibate is something he has elected to turn off, he thinks of it, understandably, as something that can just be turned on.

For the married couple physical intimacy becomes, rather, more and more an opportunity for communication, and an occasion for nurturing their relationship. Moreover, intercourse on any one occasion may be only more or less successful. Pleasure becomes increasingly a means rather than an end. In fact if pleasure is made *the* end, it becomes increasingly harder to achieve. When the personal relationship is not good, of course, intercourse is pretty much a matter of self-gratification; it is intimacy purely for self-pleasure. Under these circumstances, frequent intercourse sates the appetite for purely mechanical sex; then, the need to refrain for a ten-day span or longer may indeed revive a jaded appetite. But as the couple's relationship moves along the spectrum toward a positive, wholesome, loving one, the interpersonal elements of intercourse become so much more essential to the act that the simply personal physical pleasure grows only in proportion to the joy one is able to bring one's spouse, the mutuality of the experience, and the degree of emotional and spiritual closeness the couple feel as a result of their labors in each other's behalf. "Labors" is the right word because this success in the physical expression and cultivation of conjugal love is not easily come by. It is not just something a couple take and enjoy.

Even when a newly married couple are not making love by the calendar, are not worried about the possibility of an untimely pregnancy, or are not undergoing the psychological and physical complications of a pregnancy in process, it may take a year for the newlyweds to begin to learn how to make love to each other reasonably well. Moreover, when such a level is reached, it is not static; it takes continued efforts simply to maintain, much less grow in, the physical expression of love. The couple have the obligation to each other to do all they can to sustain mutual physical attraction and satisfaction. This requires continued conscious effort, and while the demands will vary from couple to couple, for many couples it may be very difficult. The physical relationship in marriage is not an easy one to build and retain, and it is very questionable whether one ever has the right to work at it only half of the time, if such a situation can be avoided in any other way.

Again, to speak of "giving up pleasure" as a legitimate means to family planning is grossly misleading. The pleasure that is foregone is trivial compared to the rupture in the married relationship that takes place. This suspension of intimacy not only puts a strain on the relationship during the period of temporary continence, but continues for a while when the couple resume normal relations because it builds up purely physiological pressures. After the resumption of relations, until the couple have regained what they lost during the period of estrangement, the first few experiences of intercourse revert to a more primitive level and become more lust and less love. Control is more difficult and concentration on giving pleasure to the spouse and performing a mutual act of love is lost under the build-up of purely physical needs.

There is, no doubt, a tendency for the unmarried to think of the couple not practicing rhythm as indulging in endless orgies of sex, while the couple practicing rhythm are leading a carefully rationed, controlled life of the senses. In reality the situation is quite reversed. Frequent and regular intimacy encourages control, consideration for the other, the building of subtleties into the relationship, the primacy of the relationship over the gratification. The couple that have refrained from intercourse for ten days (or perhaps five and one-half months) find it very difficult to approach intimacy in a humanly wholesome, much less sacramental way, because of the tremendous drive to relieve pent-up desire; it is almost inevitable that they will find themselves in the position of using each other for their own pleasure in spite of their best intentions.

The celibate theologian is obliged to think of sex in a depersonalized way, but a man or woman living in the sacrament of marriage is thinking of another human being and the relationship with him or her. There is a world of difference between the two viewpoints.

In some of the earlier Catholic writings opposing family planning of any kind, one can find objections against rhythm by confessors who pointed out that married couples needed the pleasures of sexual intercourse to sustain them as they met their responsibilities. This is such a niggardly, warped estimate of reality that the married couples reading such tracts must have had a strong sense of humility to avoid feelings of outrage. It is not that a couple need a little sex—like a little alcohol—to sweeten life and boost their morale with some creature comforts. It is that they need to be as close to each other as possible in every way, and physical intimacy both expresses and deepens that bond.

Moreover, it is not possible for a married couple to withdraw from each other regularly for a week or ten days at a time in one way and not withdraw to some extent in others. Looks, thoughts, experiences shared, expressions of affection that should be consciously cultivated in a healthy marriage, all must be curtailed to varying degrees. And we are not speaking here of a monastery, in which expressions of human affection are an occasionally permissible indulgence; we are talking about the family, where the cultivation of affection is a duty. (Let us not forget that there are couples who do not succeed in maintaining a sexual relationship in their marriage, even without the complication of trying to manipulate their emotions according to a calendar. And this phase of their marriage cannot be isolated from the rest of it.) And let us recall, too, that the affection quotient in a home is felt by the children as well as the adults.

Under normal circumstances these are objections one must make to the use of rhythm at all. But at certain times, rhythm seems to us especially impractical or destructive. There are many times of special strain in marriage, when couples most need to be close to each other and need all the intimacy and tenderness that can be demonstrated or evoked through conjugal love. One such time is when they have just become parents and are adjusting to their new role; their new responsibilities need the firm foundation of their original relationship with each other. With a new baby, their relationship has suddenly and subtly changed, and they must in fact undergo a new "period of adjustment." But as we have seen, for at least four and one-half months after a baby is born rhythm is impossible, and unless the couple want to risk another pregnancy before the wife has recuperated from the previous one they must practice not merely rhythm but total continence. In addition to this, the Catholic wife who wants to nurse her baby must choose between being a complete wife or a complete mother. Unlike her non-Catholic counterpart she cannot be both, unless she is husky and hardy enough to be able serenely to consider another pregnancy immediately.

When the children are small and numerous, husband and wife need, again, to be especially close. Often they are lucky if they get to speak to each other in the course of the day, about anything more personal or significant than who is going to give the baby his bedtime bath. It is not at all strange for a couple to feel that they have less chance to communicate with each other than he with his secretary and she with the pediatrician. They need to be as close emotionally, psychologically, and physically as possible in the few moments when they do have privacy. To ration their intimacy in the little time they have alone together can be desperately and insanely destructive at a time when life is hectic and they greatly need the comfort and support of their relationship, when the onslaughts are constant and there is danger of their relationship surviving at all. Under these circumstances, rhythm, even if observed, is not very effective; psychological and physiological stresses are just then affecting the wife's ovulation pattern. Total continence is really far more advisable.

About the only positive comment, then, that we find we can make about rhythm is that the negative effects rhythm has on the relationship of a husband and wife are perhaps less serious than the negative effects of too many children—that is, children too close together, or children at the wrong times.

Finally, we feel, as Catholics, that we must start to face the fact that, barring a nuclear war every twenty years to eliminate a quarter of the world's inhabitants, the population explosion is not a passing problem in our century. Family limitation is here to stay, whether we like it or not. For the welfare of the race and for the welfare of each member of our family, we feel certain imperatives. We feel the pressures of our time, not merely secular pressures, but the pressures to react in the most Christian way possible to the realities of the economic and social structure in which we live.

The national trend for earlier marriage continues. Though we may deplore that fact for many reasons, we must expect that education and the impact of mass communications (with the earlier sophistication they bring our children) are going to encourage that trend. At the same time, an economy in which there is almost no place left for the unskilled worker demands that education last longer and longer. The number of couples marrying before they have finished their schooling and can start a family is going to continue to increase. This means postponing children for the first few years of marriage. It also means more fertile years in each marriage.

Conscientious parents, it seems to us, simply cannot have as many children today as the previous generation did. They must be responsible for their children and their children's education for more years than their parents were. Living space becomes increasingly more expensive, and this is only one of the many ways in which more money, effort, and time are needed to raise each child today than were needed fifty years ago. The more we learn about the child's medical, psychological, nutritional, educative, emotional, and physiological needs, the greater becomes the parents' obligation toward the child to meet those needs. The fact that our grandparents raised ten children does not mean that today's parents of small families are slackers. What was considered adequate care of a child fifty years ago would not be adequate today. To have more children than one can give conscientious care to is an injustice to them; one must give them more than love.

Since the number of fertile years of marriage is growing and the number of children a couple can have is getting smaller, it seems inevitable at this point that rhythm is increasingly going to be *the* Catholic way of marriage. If this is true, God help the Catholic family—because we have found rhythm unnatural, unhealthy, and spiritually destructive. A parallel might be drawn. For those couples who have little good to say to each other and for whom talking is only an outlet for the ego, talking by the calendar would have little serious effect and perhaps would even be beneficial. But for the husband and wife who are truly building a marriage, intercourse is as unselfish as their conversation. The importance of the pleasure involved in intercourse is trivial compared with the importance of further building their whole relationship.

It is time Catholics stopped talking about marital love in terms of rights, indulgence, and the allaying of concupiscence. Quite clearly, a major part of the problem is that those who have been doing most of the talking (and legislating) have never tried to build a marriage. It is time we talked about making love to one's spouse as one of the essential dynamics of the married relationship, entailing as much obligation, difficulty and effort, and possessing as great an importance, as earning a living, keeping house, or raising the children. It is time we stopped thinking of sexual desire as primarily a way of seeing to it that children get conceived. Intercourse between husband and wife is an important goal in itself, and at the same time a means toward building a good, sacramental marriage in which to raise children and seek salvation.

We would like to have children in a just, charitable, and responsible fashion and to maintain a normal, whole, married relationship. And that seems almost impossible to us now.

CHAPTER FIVE

No Major Problems

Mr. and Mrs. E have had six children in nine years of marriage. Mr. E is a lay theologian; they live on the West Coast.

Mr. E writes first:

Since my profession often requires me to write on the theology of marriage, it is both harder and easier to say something about my own married life. It is harder because I cannot easily separate in my own mind my "professional" opinions and those that spring directly from my personal experience. It is easier, however, since I am somewhat used to expressing myself on sex, marriage, and family planning. But where the "is" stops and the "ought" begins I cannot, with full assurance, say.

If it were possible to sum up my professional problems on marriage briefly, I think I would choose to emphasize one thing: there is terrific pressure these days on the lay theologian and lay philosopher to do his part in urging the Church to reconsider its position on family planning and the use of contraceptives. It is taken for granted, at least in the circles in which I move, that the Church's position is defective; and that it is the duty of every honest Catholic thinker to say so in no uncertain terms.

The only way I would qualify this assertion is by adding that this pressure is as much implicit as it is explicit.

Now I suppose I can stand pressure as well as the next person. But in this instance the pressure comes from my friends, especially those who feel I might be influential should I add my voice to the chorus they would like to create. This is painful, partially because I am wary of the value of creating ground swells, and partially because I doubt that this is honest.

What is most painful, however, is that I have come to realize that many of the problems that others find so pressing have not been particularly burdensome to me. Privately, this makes me wonder whether I am an anomaly—or whether they have in fact been more influenced by the less healthy currents of secular thought than they realize. There is no way of laying to rest this kind of doubt; but my own experience may suggest why it arises.

As an adolescent, I had my share of sex problems: "self-abuse" (as the more vivid moralists like to put it); random bouts of petting; an incessant stream of lurid thoughts. For all that, I remained, technically, a virgin. Despite this latter instance of virtue (which was probably an accident since opportunity rarely knocked), a sense of guilt was part and parcel of my adolescence; if it wasn't one sexual offense it was another. Regularly I went to confession, truly repentant (or so I thought); regularly I repeated my sins. Some of my confessors were straight out of the violent literature of spoiled Catholics: hard, nasty, irascible, threatening dire things for my immortal soul. But most were kindly, understanding and patient, as if they took these things for granted. About the only consistent thing I noticed was that if one confessed to lying, anger, backbiting and sexual sins, it was inevitably the last which they talked about; the other sins—against charity—seemed to count for little.

But, in any case, marriage all but did away with those problems. I am still quite capable of having "bad thoughts" about shapely women passing me in the street, but they are infrequent and, what is more, lacking in the kind of intensity which seemed to go with youthful celibacy.

The main thing marriage taught me about sex is that it is overrated. It is a grand thing, but no more so than a dozen other experiences. I say this, I should add, from a position of pleasant marital sexual fulfillment. Sex is not a problem simply because, by virtue of a good relationship with my wife, I have come to take it as a matter of course, one more fine thing to share with my wife. Perhaps the most annoying thing about sex, in fact, is that its demands are so pressing when they can't be satisfied and the results so inconsequential when they can (leaving aside for a moment the consequence of babies).

The result of my own experience is, then, that the Church does not give one an unhealthy view of sex (though some priests do, and some laymen as well), and sex is not nearly so important as some of our latter-day Catholic romanticists would have us believe. I must confess in this latter respect that I find much of the recent Catholic speculation on the interpersonal meaning of sex more amusing than enlightening. Catholics seem forever bent on making too much of things: in the past, they made too much of the evils of sex; now they make too much of its spiritual profundities. In neither case can they seem to get the whole thing out of their minds (in this respect I don't think they realize just how trapped in the tradition they are).

Now the problem of family planning, though related to the place of sex in marriage, is a somewhat different matter. Part of the folklore of contemporary avant-garde thought is that the Church's requirement that all family planning be limited to the methods of rhythm and abstinence leads to terrible interpersonal tensions between husband and wife. I am convinced that in many cases this is true, and I have heard too many sad tales from others to dismiss their agony as the result of "secularism" or "materialism" as some simple Catholic preachers are prone to do. But I must confess that I have not found the rhythm method unbearable or wholly unreliable. Oh, it does have its tensions, but they are no worse than a dozen other tensions I experience in my work and in my ordinary marriage life. Much seems to depend upon what my general mental state happens to be at the moment. If I am working very hard, smoking too much, drinking too much coffee, wrapped up in some article or book I am writing, rhythm is no problem at all. At such times I couldn't care less about intercourse. The only times it has proved to be a problem is when I am at my leisure, when my senses are alive and there is time for play. The only snag, of course, is that it is not always easy to coordinate these things.

Most importantly, I have discovered that my desire for intercourse has little to do with any desire for a more intimate "I-thou" relationship with my wife. Instead, it seems that the two things merely coexist: sometimes the two desires arrive at the same time, sometimes not (mainly the latter). But in any case I have not found that intercourse draws me any closer to my wife than a half-dozen other things we share. I have had unhappy times with my wife when our sexual relationship was active and effective; and I have had happy times when, because of pregnancy, we observed months of abstinence. In short, I find it very hard to believe that the quality of a sexual relationship has much to do with the quality of the relationship between husband and wife (which is not to say that a bad sexual relationship could not have a very adverse effect). My own marriage has convinced me of the wisdom of those psychologists who believe that the sexual relationship is the effect of the broader husband-wife relationship and not its cause.

Now it may well be that I feel this way precisely because I have had no major problems. Though we have had six children in nine years of marriage, we have never found them too much of a burden, financially, practically, or emotionally. As far as I can judge I have been able to get as much work done as those of my friends who have fewer children. About the only difference is that they have more leisure time, and much more time to themselves. But I have got used to doing without these things. Where I seem to differ from other husbands is that I am more energetic; thus I seem to be more willing to work round the clock, to live amidst the chaos of many small children, than are a good many others. I don't see this as any special virtue, but rather a matter of temperament and physique.

Yet I would not care to suggest here that I long for a larger family. At the moment I feel my wife and I have quite enough children, and so far as I am concerned (and my wife agrees) we have done our share. The prospect of years of rhythm does not disturb me. Since it won't kill us to have another child we can stand some error in the system. Just how I would respond to a real crisis I can't guess. Perhaps I would begin railing also.

Mrs. E continues:

We may not be the first generation of Catholics attempting to sanctify sexuality in marriage, but we are certainly the first to do so in such a sex-permeated, sex-conscious society. Is the task more difficult now, or made easier by frankness and copious quantities of advice? To indulge in both, what have I learned from the concrete experience of nine years of married life?

First of all I must describe the fervent fanatical ideals which later experience was to modify. By combining the worst from the world's overestimation of sex with the worst of Catholic sentimentality I had arrived at an ideal goal that would make my marriage and family life (so I thought) an annex of heaven. Sexual relations between my husband and myself would be one long effortless ecstasy. Our union would be spiritual, passionate beyond belief, and lead us simultaneously to contemplative heights and romantic rapture. The warnings of the marriage books about overcoming inhibitions and problems of adjustment couldn't apply to *me*, for you see, I was the enlightened Christian. I knew it all—D. H. Lawrence, *Ulysses, The Hound of Heaven, Song of Songs,* and various and assorted marriage books.

So—the first lesson I learned in married life was that theory and performance are quite different. It was as though a member of the audience had bounced confidently upon the stage to perform the *pas de deux* in *Swan Lake*. How disappointing to find that the ease and coordination of perfection really did require practice! I belatedly admitted that sex was indeed an art, and tempered my expectations of being "swept away," "losing myself in the other," and so on. I might will primitive-passionate oblations, but that was no guarantee of achieving them or of obtaining orgasms.

The more I strained, yes even prayed, the less successful I was. The fatal flaw of the mind's lack of control of the body was very painful; for my sensitive, loving husband could not be fully happy if he wasn't making me fully happy and vice versa. I longed at times for a pinch of aphrodisiac. This would be better than the age-old (and ineffective) advice summed up in one word, "Pretend."

Needless to say I did not find that moralists preaching self-control in marriage were speaking to my condition. Rational self-control was the least of my problems: I needed the gift of abandonment—to relax, and freely give in to this blessed irrationality. God's gift of sex, like sleep, requires humble acquiescence to our physical body and its laws. One prays before sleep and gives thanks on awakening, but to pray *for* sleep keeps you awake. Sanctifying sex is the same. Too much spiritualizing is just one more escape from really giving yourself. As in play, the thing in itself must be done for the sake of itself. I was that unfortunate modern type mistakenly intent on using everything albeit for higher ends.

Not that I never had the opposite problem too. On occasions throughout ten years of marriage (mostly when not pregnant or nursing our six babies) I have been tempted to old-fashioned lust. In these brief times I simply wanted my own satisfactions, no matter what or who. And if I could exert power through physical desire, well all the better. But such lapses into purely sexual sins were rare; usually I (along with most women) failed marriage by selfish reluctance, by subtle sins of omission. It can all be so delicate and complex with us civilized types; the idea of simply "indulging the flesh" or "remedying concupiscence" is an anachronism (see John Updike's "Wife-Wooing"). Love is never so blatant; a real victory of charity for instance can be signaled by the slightest of provocative overtures. Rejection and withdrawal after quarrels can be equally subtle; whoever "demands their conjugal rights" anyway? The sexual relationship between husband and wife is but one part of an interweaving, fluctuating existence together.

Sex is important, yes, but it is not all-important. We have found it can create tensions and relieve tensions, but as an expression of love it is subordinate to the whole relationship. Turning the heart and mind to each other and putting his good before your own is the important thing. Mutual understanding, consideration, and a real unity of purpose can even give happiness without any sexual relationships at all. The atmosphere of our family is determined by how well we are getting along generally; sexual communion is secondary to the union of mind and will. Although sex is, by now, always perfect and one of the world's most exquisite pleasures, who has time for exquisite pleasure? Surrounded by children, never-ending work schedules and deadlines, sex really can become a luxury. My earlier romantic self would have been horrified by such an admission; I could not have guessed that increased proficiency and pleasure would accompany decreased frequency. But then, the passionate me and the everyday me are now so much one and the same person that abstinence creates no great problems. Life is so crowded and time passes so quickly that a month's abstinence now equals a day's denial of times past.

Rhythm, then, is no overwhelming problem for us. It is simply one big nuisance; I can hardly remember what day it is, much less calculate the unreliable variations of ovulation. I'm the type that needs the little battery inside that goes *bong-bong* when ovulation occurs; counting is so much trouble. All my failures with rhythm have been due really to not caring.

Once the desperate need for rest was over, then back to middle of the month intercourse; I'd always wanted a big family anyway. The real test will be from here on, for now we have just the right number for all of our family resources to be challenged but not overburdened. Yet I may have twenty years of ovulations to calculate. How dreary that prudence should require such organization!

The mention of prudence reveals the other lessons I've learned in these nine years. Inspired by the *integrity–be not solicitous* spirit, I began married life with the ideal of casting oneself upon Providence, suffering in poverty, and using rhythm only in life-and-death cases. I considered this *the* Christian approach to marriage; anyone who aspired to less was a slacker. But now, on looking back I can see the wrong premises on which I based my position, and they go like this:

(1) Whatever is most difficult to do is thereby the best and most Christian thing to do. This is always a wrong assumption, but is most dangerous in family life wherein it leads to wrong premise Number two.

(2) Suffering in family life will sanctify the family. While sacrifice may be good for adults, children need an abundance of everything. Leisure, beauty, space, material goods can't be too scarce; heroic, but fatigued frazzled parents are not good for the children. The family is no place for spiritual "brinkmanship" or letting one's spiritual eyes be bigger than one's tummy. I can see now that my own plans for relying on Providence in poverty was a form of selfish ambition rooted in pride. See how much I can suffer bravely while you soft materialists wallow in luxury! Happily this proud pose was destroyed in the most delightful fashion: money poured in on us from every side. Every new baby brought unexpected jumps in income so that willy-nilly we were catapulted into affluence. Thank goodness; the financial facts of life can be ignored for just so long. This brings me to wrong premise Number three.

(3) One should ignore the knowledge of ovulation time, ex-

cept when trying to have babies or in desperate cases. I finally realized that this was an impossible position. Once *knowing* about ovulation, I had to choose, for not choosing was really a choice in its own way. God didn't send those babies all by Himself. We were responsible for conceiving our children as well as for bringing them up. If it was a good thing to plan after a disaster, why not before? Laissez-faire family life was not intrinsically the most Christian. And so, on to Number four.

(4) The huge family living on the land is the best family vocation for all. It very soon became apparent that we were not only *not* going to end up on an obscure farm, but that we would have both gone crazy if we had. I'd rather write than bake bread, and my husband has no yen for the hoe. Twelve children would be too much for us, as well as require the sacrifice of too many other talents and ideals. All religious are not meant to be Trappists, and families too have different and valid vocations. I'm now old enough to let up on myself and admit that there are things I can do, and things that I cannot do. Now I know that everyone cannot be rigidly railroaded into the same pattern of family life. In the future we Catholics should encourage a more realistic ideal, recognizing the differences in individuals.

This ends my abbreviated account of lessons learned—but I'm still waiting to see whether the next generation will repeat the same mistakes, or find new ones all their own. An effective rhythm system will change the whole picture, but sex doesn't settle easily. Sanctifying love and family life will always be a project. Come to think of it, what am I going to learn in the *next* nine years?

CHAPTER SIX

The Difficult Decision: Contraception

Mrs. F is a twenty-six-year-old wife, mother of three children, graduate student, and part-time college professor. She lives with her family in the East.

Mr. F, also a student and teacher, concurs with her as she writes:

The topic of sexuality in marriage is just beginning to emerge from the timidity and inhibitions of the Victorian mentality, and to be discussed in a way that does justice to its nature and moral possibilities. This is true in spite of the fact that the Western world is often said to be a sex-obsessed culture where male-female relations scream at us from every magazine and TV advertisement. But this obsession is only a reaction to the puritanism and false modesty of Victorianism, and indicates that we have not yet overcome our tension and insecurity in treating of this long-hidden topic. We are trying to stifle our inhibitions by excess. The libertine is the "puritan unbound."

Both libertine and puritan fail to understand the meaning of moral maturity.

Probably our most important way of understanding the meaning of sexuality comes from our impressions of the relationship between our own mother and father. Insofar as our parents grew up in a false sexual ethos, we ourselves still suffer from it, even if by way of rebellion. In this matter, I believe that I was particularly blessed. Although my mother was brought up very much in the Victorian traditions of modesty, and always found it difficult to discuss sex with her daughters, there were very few traces of puritanism in her feelings. The relationship between my mother and father was a lifelong love affair, a fact which we took for granted as children, but the rarity of which I can now appreciate. In our home, although the topic was seldom discussed in words, we were given the feeling that sex was something very intimate and very good, the central expression of that love affair which was so evident in every aspect of the relationship between my mother and father.

There was one subject, however, on which our parents' experience gave us little hint of a solution: the subject of family planning. My parents were married when she was in her mid-thirties, and he was past forty and well-established in his career, so there was no fear lest they have children beyond their financial and psychological resources. Their fear was that they had married too late to have any children at all. Hence each of their three children were received as a joy and an unexpected gift. However, although my mother is a devout Catholic and a daily communicant, she never felt that family planning, by whatever method, was immoral. She approached family planning rather as a personal problem which people should solve without embarrassing public discussion. My mother, having had no experience on this subject herself, was most amazingly naïve about it, and my sister and I, both married at twenty and faced with quite different sorts of problems, had to work out these matters from our own rather painful experience, with little guidance from others.

In trying now to discuss the meaning of marital sexuality, I find myself somewhat overwhelmed by the inadequacies of most of the theorizing on this subject. I don't quite know why this should be, except that the subject has been so surrounded by false conceptions and mental blocks that it has made it very difficult to clear away all this tangled growth and expose its true nature, even though its true nature is by no means so abstruse and difficult to understand. Secondly, I expect this is so because a good understanding of sex is bound up with the living experience of two persons who are growing into fruition together within the framework of a permanent commitment to each other, and yet much of the discussion of sex in the past has been carried on either by celibates, who view sex with all the prejudices of their state of life, or by rakes, who view sex from the standpoint of the affair, or (in some ways the worst type of all) by medical sexologists, whose biological point of view gives us little intimation of what makes human love specifically human. This is not to say that all these people can't tell us some valid things about sex, but each when faced with the topic of sex within marriage falls into characteristic aberrations. Sex in marriage is, of all topics, the most existential; it is the topic that yields least to a kind of theorizing which does not spring from the living experience, or which springs from a different kind of living experience. It is spoken of most convincingly (at least most convincingly to me) by those who have grown over a long period of time into a mature relationship with their spouse. Being now but twenty-six and in the sixth year of marriage, I doubt that I qualify by my own standards to write on this subject, but I will try to discuss it as best I can from my present vantage point.

It has long been obvious to me that both the typical puritanical approach to sex which sees it as something rather dirty, to be condoned for the sake of procreation, and the typical sex-manual approach which sees sex as a kind of mutual masturbation, a rubbing of bodies together on a purely sensual level for the sake of some egoistic thrill, are equally misguided. This is not to say that we should overlook the physical in talking of sex, and try to find some kind of spiritualized way of talking about it (such as Christ and the Church). This kind of pseudospiritualization of sex is also an aberration and is basically just another aspect of that puritanism which regards the flesh as an unholy thing that must be redeemed by reference to disembodied realities.

Sex is the union of persons, a union of those two mirror images of humanity, man and woman. It is a union that takes place first and most importantly on the physical level, but this union is meaningless and is not in fact even really physically satisfying unless this physical union expresses the total union of these two persons on all levels of their existence. Sex is best when it is least self-conscious; when it is blissfully and even naïvely self-giving and self-forgetting. I say "naïvely" because there is a certain heresy abroad that insists that in order to "get the most" out of sex you must approach it in grim and deadly earnestness, like some sort of ordeal. I insist that we have become overpompous about this, and that is why so many people have unsatisfying sexual experiences. Sex is not work; it is play, and we have to become childish enough or simple enough to be playful. Perhaps here again we are in bondage to our puritan ancestors who early convinced us that nothing can be good and meaningful unless it is hard work. Here perhaps we can take a lesson from the Zen masters and learn that some things are achieved only when we are not striving for them; that the climax of the sexual relationship is found as a by-product of the happy, laughing, loving, self-forgetting embrace, and not as a goal in itself. The best way to miss the sexual climax is to be consciously obsessed with the need to achieve it.

On the other hand, a satisfying and developed sexual life is not achieved without art or without a long process of growth in mutual harmony and psychological accommodation. In this sense we could describe sex as a discipline, but it is not a discipline in the usual way in which this word is used; that is, some kind of chaining of the passions. What I mean by discipline is not a negating of the passions but rather the experiential growth in mutual love and harmony by which you learn to use the passions as the instruments of a beautiful orchestration of I and thou. Because marital sexuality is the point where I and thou are most poignantly expressed in order to develop a mature sexual life one must grow into increasing sensitivity to the partner's feelings, temperament, and state of soul. Each must develop an instinct for the emotional rhythms of the other. As a couple grow older in marriage, the first exuberance becomes tempered, and one tends to make love less, but it becomes more important to do it well; that is, to utilize the moments when the emotional cycles of the body, the joys and sorrows of the times, and the intimacies of the mind and spirit draw you together and call for expression in physical union.

The concepts of indulgence and abstinence seem to me to have little relevance to this discipline of the mature sexual life. It makes no more sense for the married couple to abstain from love when their emotions draw them together, than to make love when one or the other really does not feel like it, anymore than it makes sense to eat when you are not hungry or starve yourself when the body requires food. What a healthy state of body and soul requires is a balanced satisfaction of one's needs, not an excess in either direction. Some couples may make love frequently; others less frequently. This does not necessarily mean that one is "overindulgent" and the other is exercising "virtuous restraint over the passions." People's sexual drives differ in intensity. What counts is not the quantity, but the quality of the relationship. A couple may make love four or five times a week, and providing they are doing it in a way satisfying to them both, there is no reason to think that their relationship is less than wholesome. The idea that sexual relations lower a person's mental and spiritual vitality is a myth that should have been dispelled long ago. However, a couple can certainly make love too infrequently, and when persons in the prime of life have very infrequent sexual relations, the marriage is probably in emotional trouble.

Instead of ascetic notions of indulgence and abstinence, we should think in the categories of mutuality *versus* lust and physical exploitation. Genuine love is mutual self-giving. It presupposes that a couple stand on a level of personal equality with each other, that both feel that it is equally important to be loving toward the other. It is not a one-sided relationship. However, much of the traditional thinking about marriage has tended to view the relationship of husband and wife in a somewhat one-sided manner. Recently, discussions of marriage have begun to stress the necessity of sexual mutuality in marriage, but many of the older attitudes linger on, and some recent discussions of marriage by Catholic writers which I have read still assume that it is a relationship in which the woman gives and the man takes. This is not mutuality. It is exploitation, and on its lowest level it is institutionalized rape. Lust and rape are the I-it relationship instead of the I-thou relationship; they offer the kind of sexuality in which one partner, traditionally the male, simply uses the other's body as a means of self-gratification. Mature sexuality is far from lust.

To have a mature sexual life, one must purge oneself of all tendencies to simply use the other person, and one must grow into a real sense of communion. This growth is not accomplished without great restraint and discipline on the part of both partners, because sometimes one will have great sexual desire, and the other, for one reason or another, will have little or no sexual desire. Each must concede somewhat to the other. Sometimes one partner will try to arouse himself or herself to meet the desire of the other, and sometimes one will have to put down the desire in order to respect the feelings of the other. This accommodation is by no means easy to achieve because men and women are quite different in their emotional needs and rhythms, and yet it is essential if the sexual life of a couple is to be really expressive of their mutual feelings. This growth to mutuality, although it is expressed on the sexual level, obviously does not take place just on the sexual level, but it is a function of the total development of the relationship into harmony and understanding on all levels of personal existence.

Much of the current thinking on sex seems to me to ignore these larger dimensions of mutuality, and to concentrate on the level of sensual and psychological accommodation. It seems to me that while this is a great improvement over the Victorian attitude which regarded the woman as simply the passive vehicle of the man's desire, it is still too superficial. Man and woman have minds and spirits, and mature sexuality should express mutuality on these levels as well. I think it is not too much to say that if a couple are not really communicating with each other on the deepest levels of their mind and spirit, their sexual life will soon run into trouble. Yet current popular thought seems to see little relevance of this continuing intellectual and spiritual growth which the couple share with each other and inspire in each other. The average American couple today all too often live in different worlds and are expected to live in different worlds, and the daring woman who crosses over the invisible barricade at a gathering, to join the "men's" conversation, is taking her reputation in her hands. The wife is expected to be caught up in a world of babies and wife-talk and to be fully satisfied in these interests. The husband is expected to live in a world of men and events. Man and woman are supposed to have little interest or contact with the world of the other. Obviously, a couple living in such a schismatic state will find their ability to communicate limited to the routines of daily life. To me this is a shocking and dangerous situation.

Communication on the level of intellectual interests and concerns should be the life's blood of a growing personal relationship; yet few people seem to apply this to marriage and realize that shared passions and shared purses are not enough. There is no enduring love which is not founded upon friendship. Certainly the dissatisfaction of the many married couples that I know springs in large part from this breakdown in communication, this lack of shared intellectual worlds and shared intellectual interests. My husband and I have an advantage in both being students with many intellectual interests in common. Through all financial difficulties, emotional strains and crises, one of the basic bonds between us is the very simple fact that we have so much to talk about, so many ideas to discuss with each other. Is it not time to abandon the traditional anti-intellectual bias toward the roles of wife and mother, and realize that the woman's intellectual development, far from being an unnecessary appendage or even a detriment to her roles, is one of the most essential ways in which the relationship between husband and wife can be more than such a biological or a socioeconomic bond, but truly the bond of I and Thou?

Having discussed what the sexual life can and should be as an expression of the total union of man and woman, let us then ask how the attempt to live according to the Church's precepts of "chaste" fertility control coincides with, or is conducive to, a mature sexual life. It is evident to most married people that the sexual act as an expression of love and the sexual act as an act of procreation, while biologically identified, are two separate and very distinct purposes as far as psychology and personal intentionality are concerned. In order to create both a harmonious sexual life and a happy and willing spirit of maternity and paternity, it is necessary or at least highly desirable that these two purposes be under such control that they can be separated or united according to the actual intentions of the couple, and that this control be achieved by a method which is both fully effective and conducive to psychological naturalness; that is, a method which does not obstruct the emotional rhythms of a healthy sexual life. Under the Church's present attitude toward sex and fertility control, this ideal is very difficult and, at least as far as our own experience is concerned, impossible to attain.

We found it impossible to use the rhythm method without fatally destructive consequences to our sexual relationship. Now it should be evident that the time when married couples could live like the birds and the bees with little concern for the number of children they produced is irrevocably past. The pressure of our present commitments to society and to each other dictate a concern for family planning at the very outset of marriage. Our experience, and I know the experience of many other Catholic couples, indicates that the Catholic who tries to achieve fertility control will have to sacrifice much in his sexual relationship, so much in fact that in many cases we must conclude that requirements for a full and satisfying sexual life have been destroyed.

There are a number of reasons why the attempt to follow the Church's views on this subject creates an almost insuperable obstacle to the healthy emotional dynamics of the sexual relationship, and I shall try to illustrate these from our own experience. When a couple is first married, even though they may think they know each other pretty well, they can scarcely imagine though how little they really know each other and how much personal growth is required before they can really begin to mesh with each other's temperaments. Therefore, it is highly desirable that a young couple have a year or two at the beginning of marriage to deepen their personal relationship, before they shoulder the additional strain of pregnancy. The average young couple is simply not ready for parenthood in the first year of marriage. In our case, I think this might have been particularly important because my husband and I, although we have a tremendous field of common interests and values, are temperamentally quite different. I am the nervous explosive type and he the meditative one who has difficulty bringing his deepest feelings to the surface. In addition, we come from very different social backgrounds, in spite of our common religion, and in our first years of marriage we were scraping along on the minimal existence provided by a graduate fellowship.

The Church in general does not recognize the validity of this period of growth before the birth of children, and frowns on any attempt at birth control until the couple are properly desperate and inundated with off-spring. The reason for this, implicitly if not explicitly, is that birth control at the beginning of marriage, within the Church's precepts, is practically impossible. Anyone who has the slightest knowledge of the dynamics of sexuality knows that the successful use of rhythm is virtually beyond the reach of any newly wed couple. Perhaps we have here little more than an attempt to make a duty out of a necessity. Recognizing that it is almost impossible to "program" your sexual relations in the first year of marriage, it perhaps seems expedient to insist that the couple are sinning unless they procreate immediately. (We were told, quite gratuitously, by my husband's pastor on our first visit to him that if we did not have a child within a year, he would know that we were "living in sin.") Yet it is difficult to ignore or to deny the obvious value of this growing period at the beginning of marriage, a value which is generally recognized and promoted by marriage counselors. It is quite evident to us both that we would have gotten off to a much better start in our married life if such a growing period had been possible. Our marriage is still suffering from the residue of misunderstanding that could have been surmounted in the first year or two, if we had not immediately been plunged into the additional anxieties of parenthood.

However, somehow one manages to survive anything, and soon after the birth of our first child we moved out of our one-bedroom carriage house, with newspapers stuffed in the cracks to keep out the weather, into a solid structure which more adequately deserved the name of "shelter." Since my husband was still a student with no income except a scholarship, we embarked in earnest upon the attempt to achieve some kind of rational fertility control. So concerned were we with this prime necessity that we scarcely thought of the effect that this was having upon our on-going emotional life. After two more children were born in fairly quick succession, it was evident that despite our use of the best scientific aids available, and our rigid channeling of our sexual relations, no effective control could be had with the rhythm method. We followed the rules, but the rules were not good enough.

But by that time we had had sufficient experience to realize that this farcical attempt to control nature by insufficient means was destroying the emotional life that underlay our marriage. We realized that the rhythm method is in such direct contradiction to the natural emotional rhythms of man and wife, and was forcing us to live under such a regime of anxiety, tension, and dissatisfaction that our whole marital life was on the verge of turning into something very cold and angry. I found that after repeated experience with the inadequacies of the method I began to be terrified of the sexual act and that this was making it almost impossible for me to give myself freely and fully. During the time of abstinence I would feel, however, great pangs of sexual longing; then when the "safe period" arrived, my sexual desire seemed to fade away, and I would become fearful and shrink from the sexual act. I gradually began to realize that this was more than a fear-inspired frigidity, and that the use of rhythm was also in direct contradiction to my natural cycle of sexual emotion, which should (and I have since had this confirmed by good medical authorities) properly be at its height during the middle of the cycle and fade away toward the end. (Women, of course, experience individual differences both in the nature of this emotional cycle and in their perception of it.) In any case it became evident to me that the practice of rhythm was depriving us of even the elementary possibility of a wholesome sexual life. Since I felt a great need to satisfy my husband's desires and to show him that I loved him, I tried to force myself to make love during the "safe period" and pretend that I enjoyed it, but it is impossible to feign feelings on that level of intimacy. Finally, when I was carrying our third child, it became clear to us both that we had reached the end of our rope, and we could no longer live under such a biological tyranny. I think I can truly say with all candor that as far as our viability as human beings was concerned, there was no alternative but to seek some method of birth control which did not create such conflicts and was better suited to its purpose.

Having crossed this bridge some months ago, what now can be said, from this new vantage point, of sexual maturity and family planning? Is it that much better? Has everything suddenly been transformed into bliss? We hardly expected such miracles. All we really hoped for was the elementary possibility of living a normal emotional life. The ability to relax with each other, to no longer feel the calendar hanging over our heads like an ax, this was sufficient reward. It is also clear that far from being able to mature sexually during these first six years of marriage, something has set us back tremendously, and it will undoubtedly take us some time before we can fully repair the ravages that have been wrought upon our emotional lives.

The first few months after our decision I think I was a little bit stunned by it all, like a prisoner that has been let out of a dark hole and is getting used to the sunlight. It took awhile to realize that I no longer needed to be afraid; I could relax and laugh and love as we had done when we were first married.

I also realized that I had been living in a state of suppressed rage for five years, a rage at trying to conform to standards that were an insult to my intelligence and my feelings. Perhaps this is why one writes articles. It is a way of getting certain kinds or wrath out of your system. It may then seem that I have been talking of an ideal of mature sexuality which we have not achieved at all, and yet I think we have suffered and loved enough to know what it should be and can be, and in a certain sense we feel that we have been given a fresh start and that much growth is possible now that we are able to put the forces of biological nature within some properly humanized framework. For the first time, we can feel free to embrace when our feelings and psychological rhythms really draw us together, instead of trying to turn ourselves off and on in some mechanized fashion. Now we are free to create a child when we are ready for it, in a joyful and positive manner, instead of expending all our energies in trying to stem the full force of some inevitable avalanche.

Doubtless there will be many who will wish to belittle our experience and condemn our decision, but from our point of view there seems no avoiding another kind of value-judgment. Surely a valid method of family planning should not be such as to destroy a healthy marital life. This is to cut off one arm to save another. Surely genuine Christian values must be built upon genuine human values and not upon their denial or destruction. Is it too much to suggest that where human needs and human feelings are given a healthy respect, we cannot be far from a valid Christian understanding of marriage, sexual maturity, and family planning?

CHAPTER SEVEN

Husband First

Mr. G is a financial officer in the government of a North-western state; he and Mrs. G, after fifteen years of marriage, are the parents of a daughter, thirteen, and five sons between the ages of twelve and one.

Mrs. G writes:

I recall a stormy, early winter afternoon not long after our wedding; my husband returned from a hunting trip, dripping wet and cold, but with some fine birds for our Sunday dinner. We were to go out later that evening, and after his shower he suggested we take a nap. The northern winter darkness had already descended and outside the wind raged against the old house we lived in, hurling the rain against the windowpanes. We were literally thousands of miles away from our old homes, embarked on a new life in a strange land; yet the contrast of our island of bliss in the midst of the storm and darkness is a time I have never forgotten. And so our marriage started.

I am one of those who thinks that the sexual union is life's greatest experience. I thank God for it, along with all His other

blessings, and to me it is symbolic, not only of God the creator
but also of God the lover. Love is both gift and goad, for it
urges us, almost irresistibly, to take up the burdens of thirty
years or more of all-encompassing responsibility which even
the raising of a small family entails, and a lifetime of mona-
gamy, and it rewards us with the greatest of treasures.

My husband and I never felt any need to buy marriage
manuals. I decided from the start that my husband is the
world's greatest lover, and while the passing of the years makes
the expression of our love a little less frequent, it is just as
eager and perhaps even more tender and delightful than at
the start. I don't think we ever concerned ourselves with "adjustment"; good lovers pursue each other, it seems as simple
as that. But I have often wondered if the sexual union, which
is the perfection of a good marriage, is not the salvation of
many a mediocre marriage.

The scales of matrimony are heavily weighted by responsibility; the joys of the sexual union make up a most important
part of the counterbalance. For every ode to the firstborn son
there are a dozen honoring the love of his father for his mother;
nevertheless, another great balance-weight is the natural tender
love we feel toward our children.

If I had twelve children, instead of six, or if nature had
ordained that a woman might occasionally bear thirty instead
of about twelve, I am sure the twelfth or the thirtieth would
be as cherished as the first. We need not be instructed or
admonished to cherish our children, to regard them as treasures and jewels; we already know they are—it is written on
our hearts. As the biologist Loren Eisely has said, man has
survived not because he is tough-minded, but because he is
tender-minded. Men care tenderly for their pregnant wives,
and women care tenderly for their helpless children. To a
mother, every detail of her baby, his face, his expressions, the
first steps and the first words, the unfolding of the infant
intelligence—all are observed with the greatest of fascination.

And how proud we parents are as our children progress through childhood; the first book read, a sport mastered, a son serving at the altar, the first money earned by baby-sitting or on a paper route.

There is a very intense mother-child relationship during the toddler stage which I must emphasize because we have had a toddler at our house for a dozen years, except for a brief period between our third and fourth sons. At this age, during the second year of life particularly, the child is his mother's master and owner. No one else on this earth is loved with such possessive love as the mother of a toddler. When his mother holds him in her arms, his fingers explore her mouth, her teeth and tongue; he discovers therefrom and with delight that he too has a tongue and a few teeth. He pulls her hair and twists her nose; after about a year of this he is convinced that the nose is not going to come off and gets bored with his mother's face, his first great exploration in the world.

Natural tenderness alone does not get through to the tired, overworked mother; her peevish, whining toddler may be temporarily quite unattractive. Then courage is the virtue that counts most, based, of course, on a good Christian philosophy of life, or at least on some stable philosophy of life. Needless to say, if a mother had preschool children aged one, two, three and four, and is perhaps great with child number five, these difficult times are even more frequent. When the children sprout up round the table like green olive plants, and one's quiver is full of sons, gracious living goes out the window, not to return for many years.

I love the bondage, yet I long for release too; nor do I feel any shame or guilt over such a conflict of feelings, for what mother has not said, "Thank God, he's out of diapers!" or "Thank God, he's started to school!"

Besides the rewards of sexual love and the love we feel for our children, I have found most rewarding the companionship and the good times we have, just as husband and wife, and as a family, and the security and stability that come with stable family life. Still, it is the sexual union, the essence of marriage, and the love of the children which come first, for these other rewards might be found in other human relationships, even perhaps in the religious life.

The daily grind of family life to keep the troop fed and watered and freshly laundered and bedded down is not very glamorous but very essential, and actually the bulk of family life is devoted to such tasks. After this comes the character and social training, a much more difficult task and with less guarantee, especially in these times, of success. All parents have to face it: lies are told, change is stolen, parental laws are at times impudently disobeyed, twelve-year-old daughters develop a sudden interest in sailors, big brothers bully little brothers, insults are hurled, arrows are shot through windows, and couch cushions are slit by bowie knives ("But I was only wrestling sharks, Mom"); toilets are left unflushed, and soup is slurped. All must be dealt with, coped with, muddled through; sometimes with righteous wrath and swift justice, at other times with careful training, patience, perseverence, and love, and then more of the same. My temper is much more apt to flare at the count of two times two, rather than the scriptural injunction to seventy times seventy, so the sweetness-and-light technique is particularly difficult for me.

It is still frequently advanced that one advantage of a large family is that the older ones will help with the younger ones. Although the same amount of energy is usually required to cajole him into doing the work as the task itself requires, a well trained twelve-year-old can indeed be a great deal of help. This is due to the dreary fact that almost any household task, with the exception of the higher culinary skills, can be performed by said well trained twelve-year-old. Children are virtually no help at all, however, before the age of nine or ten, so the mother who bears her children one right after the other is faced with no assistance for at least ten years.

We do not feel it is fair to demand more than half an hour of help on weekdays or one hour on Saturdays from our older children, and of course the younger ones must start with tasks that take only a few minutes. Our daughter often has two hours of homework at night from her accelerated class; she is up at 7 a.m. and walks a mile to school so she can be in band practice at eight; she is also active in Girl Scouts and baby-sits, usually one night each weekend, to earn money. Our oldest boy has less homework but is in Scouts, serves as altar boy at 7 a.m. Mass one week a month, and on Sundays and special occasions is a substitute on a paper route, and is all out for skiing during the winter months. Most teenagers have just such busy schedules, and while it is right to insist that they carry their share of the family chores, it does not seem fair to ask much more. I know personally of two large families where the oldest daughter is the family servant; such a situation is not just.

Before leaving the subject of family work, I might mention that the most common complaint I hear from wives, or which I have observed in the families of my friends, is that husbands all too often offer little or no help, either in home maintenance or in child rearing. The mother of several children, especially when there are preschool children, must work sixty to seventy hours a week; the husband usually works a forty-hour week and has vacations and sick leave. The resentment when the husband offers little or no help is, I think, often quite justified and understandable. Very few mothers have any real vacation and the only total sick leave comes with childbirth, or hospitalization with 104-degree fever or a broken leg. Lesser afflictions, including morning sickness, must be borne by the mother, resting if she can between essential duties which drag her from her bed to change the babies' diapers, make another peanut butter sandwich, hang up the washing, sweep up the cereal and sugar that has been spilled on the kitchen floor, or stop the toddler from playing in the toilet.

When the husband is in one of the more demanding profes-

sions or in business for himself, he may also of course be working a sixty- or seventy-hour week, or commuting may keep him
from home ten hours a day. Then the complaint of the wife is
that she never sees her husband, except when he is ready to
fall asleep, and that he has no time for his family and their
life together.

The problem of the wife going to work often arises, too,
not necessarily out of any desire on her part to get away from
the home, but from the sheer force of financial necessity when
the medical bills mount over the thousand-dollar mark, the
house needs a new roof, and the car is too ancient to maintain
any longer; unfortunately, such things can all happen within
the same year. I am stoutly opposed to mothers of preschool
children taking on forty-hour-a-week employment except in
cases of dire necessity, but because dire necessity does sometimes raise its head, I would like to see some Catholic action
aimed at achieving "mothers' hours" for women in the labor
force. Many jobs could be made available on a twenty-hour-a-
week basis, or a working day from 9 a.m. to 3 p.m. for mothers
of school children, or even one- or two-day-a-week jobs.

We are now comfortably off financially, but during the earlier
years of our marriage, when we had four little ones and my
husband was on a clerical level rather than an administrative
one, all these duties had to be performed on a per capita income
that would not support the local convent. Our economies have
included Army surplus lemonade powder, day-old bread, rum-
mage-sale clothes, and countless hours of do-it-yourself repairs
to a forty-five-year-old house. I know for many people the
financial problem is never any easier, but for all of us it is a
greater problem in this century than in the last. For instance,
medical care that is an essential today did not even exist in
the last century; people were born at home, were ill at home,
and died at home. Too, the higher education which we must
encourage and support was a rare thing indeed a century ago,
and a few centuries before that it was quite possible to be a

happy and productive illiterate. Today it is deemed rather
hopeless to be a high school drop-out. The daughter who once
married at fifteen now marries at twenty, and the son who
once went to work at twelve or fourteen now starts his career
at eighteen, twenty-two, or even later.

Our constant anxiety is not over financial problems, even
though these can be difficult enough on a comfortable income,
nor even over physical safety, which is a great concern in itself
with five lively boys. It is most of all over character development and training. We want to transmit values to our children;
we want them to care about what we care about, to hold important what we hold important, and even to despise what we
despise. We want them to be good, to be strong and resource-
ful, to use their intelligence, to be happy and productive, to be
warm and loving. We want them to have good taste and to
recognize and love what is beautiful and true. Last but certainly
not least, we want them to know, love and serve God, and to
obey the commandments.

It is these things, the most difficult and worrisome of all our
duties, which we discuss the most frequently, and it is in this
area that we most often feel we have made mistakes. It is such
a big job. Communication of ideas and ideals is always somewhat difficult, and it is never so difficult as between the generations.

The great blessing of sexual compatibility which we have had
from the start of our marriage has been offset by difficulties
in limiting family size. I was twenty-seven when we married
and when my first child was born I was twenty-nine. We hoped
to have four children, but as we wanted them spaced, we
made use of the rhythm system after the birth of the first child
and in the subsequent years of our marriage. This resulted in
the fourth child being born by the time the eldest was four
and a half. By then some of the usual saggy, baggy health
problems made it imperative to stick to our original intention
about family size. So, with faith and hope we started a practice

of very strict periodic abstinence, but during the next six years two more children were born to us. During this period I had the services of very competent medical men at my disposal, one of them a Catholic physician; all were willing to give advice on the rhythm system although they warned me about its limited effectiveness. One of my doctors, whom I questioned about any recent advances in the temperature method for determining ovulation time, replied that he thought that was a great deal to ask of a thermometer.

Perhaps this will suffice to explain my rather jaundiced view of the rhythm system. Except for the two intervening pregnancies, for many years we abstained for all but five or six days at the end of every month, and practiced total abstinence for as long as five months at the birth of the last children. A woman would understandably become disgruntled if after sticking to a strict 1200-calorie diet she gained ten pounds; so here.

Looking back with the degree of objectivity that comes with early middle age, I must say that a system that demands three weeks abstinence out of every month and five months total abstinence at the time of childbirth is much too harsh, even if it was successful. Even so, I would not feel such total disenchantment with the method if (1) it worked, and (2) its exclusive acceptance did not raise serious intellectual problems.

It is only natural that thoughful married people would reflect on the meaning and purpose of sex; marriage is, after all, our sacrament. As responsible parents and citizens we must prudently evaluate any number of issues great and small, and act, judge, or vote accordingly. It is scarcely to be expected that we would dismantle our intelligence and stow it in the bedroom closet when the question is the proper use of sex or the population explosion. I believe that the knowledge of the natural law is a product of human reason alone, and that adherence to its doctrine, far from relieving us of the burden of thought, intensifies the need for it. Thus it is even possible to hope that the reflections of married people on the married state may be considered in interpretations of the natural law, not as votes to be counted but as evidence to be weighed.

As a prayerful setting for the use of reason I am particularly fond of the Collect of the sixth Sunday after Epiphany; "Grant, we beseech Thee, almighty God, that ever pondering on reasonable things, we may accomplish both in words and works, that which is pleasing in Thy Sight." The long and beautiful Psalm 118 is another favorite of mine for meditation. We must possess our vessels in holiness; is it only a romantic notion to wish they might be brimming over with the good wine of life, instead of empty or half full?

The sexual union is regarded universally as the essence of marriage, the one thing that sets marriage apart from all other human relationships. If the sexual union is not universally regarded as the pearl of great price, certainly it is held to be such by the largest number of mankind.

Yet sooner or later so many married couples find themselves impaled on the horns (one might better say antlers, there are so many facets to the problem) of the awful dilemma that demands choice between sacrificing the health of the mother and/or the security of the family, disobeying the laws of the Church, or throwing away the pearl of great price.

Such problems are bound to bring forth long, long thoughts, accompanied by anguish of soul. It can be a holy suffering, as Karl Adam describes in *The Spirit of Catholicism*. It is not, however, just a question of what we ourselves may be able to bear or how we are going to solve the problem; it is also a question of what our children are to do in their marriages, and what the whole human race is to do.

My own intellectual difficulties stem firstly from the fact that all methods of controlling conception are artificial (the rhythm system might just as well be called an artificially patterned marital relationship). Furthermore, all methods have as their honest purpose the nullification of the possibility of conception in the sexual union and the retention of the marital relationship in as integral a way as possible. Nor are the intellectual difficulties lessened by the approval and recommendation of a method of sexual brinkmanship, which, whatever it may be as a sexual practice, involves intellectually a full blown element of sophistry.

It is now known that about 10 percent of all married couples have a sterile union, and another 10 percent have such low fertility that they bear only one or two children; yet we do not even know how many of the remaining 80 percent find rhythm adequate, or how many find it totally unreliable.

We can be sure, however, that all too many Catholic couples are faced with a choice, not of contraception or control but of contraception or total abstinence. Total abstinence indeed! That blight upon the marriage bed, flattering only to the frigid, and consoling only to the incompetent! Excessive tampering with normal behavior is no wiser than excessive tampering with normal physiology. Delayed marriage, periodic abstinence, and total abstinence, as methods of conception control, should be submitted to the same careful analysis and evaluation which any method of contraception must undergo.

The second intellectual difficulty revolves around the natural purpose of sex itself. The textbook answer is that the primary purpose is procreation. Yet I do not think that we, or probably any other couple, even at those times when children are hoped for, enter into sexual intercourse thinking about it as a procreative power. A young couple in love marry, if they are not just arranging or accepting a marriage of convenience, because they desire each other, need each other, and can scarcely wait to possess each other. Their desire for children may be strong, but it is the lesser motivation. I think most married people would agree that from the start sex in marriage has a value of its own, quite apart from its procreative possibilities. The greater the gifts of love, the greater the value is placed on them, so that one may truly say that sexual love is the greatest experience of life.

Or, to look at it in a more scientific manner, one may observe that the sexual relationship in marriage does not end with pregnancy or lactation or the menopause, nor is it confined to the fertile period of the month. The menstrual cycle itself physiologically differs from the estrus cycle of lower mammals in most significant ways, for it permits the use of sex, the right and proper use of the marital relationship, far in excess of its procreative function. Indeed, as a reproductive act the sexual union is successful less than one percent of the time, if one considers twenty years as an average for the childbearing period of marriage. Conception, which holds undisputed primacy of purpose as a result of the sex act among lower animals, must share and eventually yield its place. Our sexuality makes us not more like the lower animals but less like them.

It seems to me that the sexual union has the function of conception, which is meant to be occasional, and the function, which is meant to be permanent, of the formation and maintenance of monagamous marriage. Both functions serve the same ultimate purpose, that of the preservation of our species. Ancient mammalian maternity is joined by paternity in its fullest sense only with human beings, and I have come to believe that the permanent sexual relationship is a prerequisite of monagamous marriage, just as a lifetime marriage contract is necessary to the preservation of a species whose offspring have such a prolonged period of infancy and dependency.

My reflections on these matters, however, do not always follow the course of logic, for I must admit to a burning rage when I see women suffering, and one need not look far: my friend in her early forties with ten living children, suffering a miscarriage with serious after-effects; an acquaintance, a young mother in our parish with four children, recently returned from her second stay in a mental hospital, where her doctors warned her against bearing any more children; yet she is psychologically unable to bear the conflict between this advice, that of her confessor, and the demands of her husband.

Again, there are the several young women I know, still in their mid-twenties and pregnant with their fifth child in five years; and the women whose veins deteriorate more and more with each successive pregnancy.

As far as we women are concerned, there is a jagged gash in the breastplate of justice, and there are too many broken plumes on the helmet of salvation. The suffering might all be justified in face of a declining population; in the face of a population explosion, it is not. The injustice of the situation is that those under the most stress, and usually those couples who are bearing the greatest responsibility (reproductive responsibility, by the way, for what else is the rearing of children than a reproductive responsibility) must also make the greatest sacrifice of their marital rights. The Sabbath is still made for man, and not man for the Sabbath, yet there is no equity here, no matter how many frail women are dashed against the rocks of these hard sayings.

I have a good friend with seven children who quips that she wouldn't worry so much about the population explosion if it would just stop exploding at her house. Bad as our own immediate problems are, it would be simpler if we could concern ourselves only with the size of our own families. There is, however, also the question of what to teach our own children, since it now appears that the birthrate will keep ahead of the death rate, with three or less children as a family average. We must also decide for ourselves, and later on discuss with them, the political questions involved in the control of world population. We feel zealous concern, not indifference or disbelief, about the fact that population will double in many places in the world in as little as eighteen years and that 45 percent of the population of many Central and South American countries are under the age of fifteen, and being cared for by an adult population which is from 50 to 90 percent illiterate.

Yet what help for high fecundity can we Catholics offer either to our own children or to the poor married couples who live in huts around the world but that leaky rowboat of the rhythm system, whose users vainly search through the mists for the monthly appearance of the North Star, which stubbornly refuses to lend itself to astronomical observation and prediction. True, we are going to patch up the craft (we might even add a motor), we are going to find the North Star, but St. Thomas' observation that the art of sailing governs the art of shipbuilding is as true today as it was in the thirteenth century. Let us get our doctrine of sexuality in marriage straight, before passing judgment on the arts made possible by science.

Contrary to a belief generally implied by advocates of control, married couples do not, even when the opportunity presents itself, act in some bacchanalian fashion. I insist we are not selfish slobs for preferring sex on Saturday to sex on Tuesday—and every third Tuesday at that. The iron traces of our daily life impose a discipline of their own, on which the rhythm system must be superimposed.

Consider a not untypical situation in our family. On Saturday afternoon the children are finally variously distributed at a matinee, a Scout hike, or down for a nap. Mother and father have a quiet lunch together, love is inviting, but the safe period doesn't start until Tuesday. On Tuesday night, father must attend a Boy Scout Court of Honor and we fall on our twin beds exhausted by a twelve-hour day. Almost every morning there is a small son in bed with one of us, usually complete with wet diapers. Wednesday, the federal auditors arrive in fathers' department for their annual visit and stay the rest of the week. Saturday, mother is nursing three children ill with sore throats, and by Monday another cycle comes to its normal but dramatic conclusion; an event, incidentally, which is hailed with delight, especially if a few days late.

There are, of course, those blessed times when the desire, the opportunity, and the safe period all coincide. But what parents have not been interrupted on a trip to the Promised Land by the banging of little fists on the bedroom door and a loud and insistent wailing for mommie?

The language of desire is easily drowned out by fatigue, tension, or illness, and it requires privacy. It needs, at times, to be fostered and nurtured rather than controlled. After an illness it is a sign of returning health and strength; after a setback in life or a family crisis it can restore peace and return the joy of living.

Since variation is as typical of human beings as uniformity, it is not surprising that one may now read considerable diversity of opinion from married people themselves, at least as it is reported in the Catholic press. No doubt many years will pass before we find solutions to these problems, although in the matter of the population explosion we have only decades, not centuries, in which to operate. I like to consider St. Paul's Epistle to the Romans, Chapter 14, as pertinent to our dilemma, although then the early Christians were concerned with food and drink and the day of the Sabbath, and whether Jewish converts should become Gentile or Gentile converts should be Jewish. So if my sister wishes to be careful, let her be so, for the Lord. And if my sister wishes to cast her cares upon the Lord, let her be careless, for the Lord. And if I, having borne six children, wish to use sex for love's sake, let me do so for the Lord, and giving thanks to God.

CHAPTER EIGHT

Learning to Love

Mr. and Mrs. H live in the East, where Mr. H teaches. They have been married five years, and have three children.

Mrs. H begins:

We came to marriage just six months and two years after our respective receptions into the Church, and the illusions which we brought to it erred principally on the side of spiritual naïveté. During the period of our conversions our energies had been directed toward defending to ourselves and to others the Church's teaching on birth control. Not only had we little insight into its practical difficulties, but we fondly imagined ourselves the parents someday of five or six children. We write now at our fifth anniversary, and we can marvel that while the past five years have presented an unrelenting procession of corrections for such sentimentalities, their destruction of the unreal in us has been kind, leaving our real capacities unharmed and more clearly defined.

My husband and I met while we were in neighboring, small secular colleges. My conversion to Catholicism from the Episcopal church climaxed a childhood of unusual religious preoccupations (discounting the psychological functions they served). I entered the Church at the beginning of my college career. My acquaintance with Kenneth began coincidentally, about one and one-half years later, when he was preoccupied with turbulent religious ideas and impulses which had become important for him only after he had entered college. I was for him, at first, simply an articulate contact with Catholicism. After he had formed his commitment to the Church, our relationship remained and became what had been furthest from my mind in the beginning—an engagement. After such a relationship it was natural that goals which we thought of as spiritual headed our list of purposes in marrying. These included a rosy colored view of the probable results of the use of rhythm, when it might become necessary as a means of family limitation. From this period also came the illusory feeling that we were absolutely one in our attitudes toward religious practice. This has been true, of course, in undoubted fundamentals: we have clearly placed our entire marriage within the context of its relationship to God and to his Mystical Body. But our sense of unity at first obscured the necessity of facing the vast difference in our pre-Catholic religious and psychological backgrounds.

We seemed to find no hint of these differences in the enthusiasm of our first year or so (when, for instance, we saw our way to becoming professed in a Third Order whose rule now seems hardly compatible with our complicated life), but now they are appearing on all sides to reveal our painfully different, real religious temperaments. My desire for considerable overt devotion, bolstered by both valid and invalid childhood habits, runs continually counter to Kenneth's inclination to try to find his most meaningful relationship to God in the daily realities of his life as husband, father, and scholar-teacher without much added effort in the direction of conventional piety. I realize that this may be largely a general problem of masculine-feminine focus, but it presents a most perplexing

division in the area where we want to be most united. I don't
know quite where this puzzle is tangent on our problems of
sexuality, but since the two are so often mingled in my emotional
reflections, I don't want to ignore it entirely.

Our awareness of the intricacies of using periodic abstinence
was hardly formed until after the birth of our first child and
was not really experienced until the recent reestablishment of
my menstrual cycle after our third child's birth. At the time
of our wedding we were not instructed on the method of
determining the date of ovulation by the cycles of body temperature, and we had nothing to rely on but the calendar-
count. Our first conception occurred about a month after the
wedding, probably because we far underestimated the number
of days of continence needed (as I remember, we depended on
a four-day interruption). The pregnancy and six months of the
nursing period provided a temporary holiday from the demands
of rhythm, a happy circumstance, actually, for the first year of
marriage. Tension returned after a few months of lactation,
but the first ovulation passed without conception while I was
still nursing. We discovered the temperature cycle and were
able to chart for two months a recognizable rise following
ovulation. Still, we did not learn to extend the abstinence to a
length of maximum safety. We thought of the method, in fact, as
a means of reducing abstinence to a minimum, and as a result,
a simple mistake about the day's date produced our second
little boy. Again we were relieved of anxiety for eighteen months.
(This time the cycle did not appear until a month after weaning, in the baby's ninth month.) We were grateful in both
cases for the relative safety of the first half of lactation, because
it would have been very hard to move from the three-month
abstinence required medically (six weeks before and after
birth) to immediate concern about conceiving again.

Our attitudes toward the first two births during pregnancy
were happily tolerant. It wasn't supposed to happen this way,
but we were managing. We had generous financial help from

parents throughout my husband's two years of part-time graduate study. I had been able to do enough work to insure the
completion of my master's degree (which I had begun on a fellowship the year we married). I fully enjoyed pregnancy and
was fortunately prepared for natural childbirth, which Kenneth
and I were able to experience together in an unusual hospital.
Our babies were delightful and I delighted in nursing them.
We had no medical difficulties.

By the return of menstruation after the second birth, it was
hard to be unconcerned about the possibility of further pregnancies. Kenneth had just begun his first year of full-time teaching. The dissertation had been planned out, but the end was
nowhere in sight. The ultra-conservative institution that had
hired him made his teaching experience frustrating, but full-
time work was now necessary no matter how long it delayed
his Ph.D. We were spending a disproportionate amount of our
income to provide a decent apartment in suburban Washington,
D.C. (meaning one large enough to provide room to study),
and we were beginning to feel the imprisonment of young
parents who cannot move without a hired baby-sitter.

From my point of view there was one overwhelming fact
about the children relevant to their mother: neither of them
ever learned automatically to sleep through the night. At that
time, it had been nearly two years since I had slept a full
night. Even more crucial was the transition of our first boy
from babyhood to his third year. I was becoming shocked by
the difference in my reactions to the child as a baby and as a
demanding, and to me, often revolting, two-year-old. My emotional sympathy went out entirely to his contrasting baby
brother, for whom he naturally felt rivalry. I began to realize
with panic that mothering a baby (with whom I had never
been angry no matter what its physical demands) was easy,
because the baby appealed to my own emotions, while the
raising of a child required a disinterested charity of which I
obviously had almost none. And I seemed to find little means

of arousing that charity since it was really the destruction of the image of myself that depressed me wildly as I "watched" myself dispense a sinful degree of physical violence to my child because I couldn't stand his incorrigible habit of nose-picking.

Now I began to view with intense irony and near despair my complacent assumption that I could easily raise a sizable, "Catholic-type" family because I had proved myself in school a competent person. I found that I knew nothing of the unconditional love between parent and child in which God's relationship with man is mirrored. What I had when I thought I had love was a sentimental, idealized picture of childhood. I had thought a great deal about the possibilities for a child's spiritual education, but I had not faced the necessity to love him when he disgusted me. The lovelessness of my own family experience began to fit into the picture of my own unpreparedness; I could no longer toss it off with a pious condemnation. When I read now in newspapers of child-murder in passion, I don't feel indignant as I once would have, but I feel instead an agonized sympathy for the parent because I know that I have not been above sharing the impulse. I say this only to emphasize the change in perspective as a parent which I experienced during by oldest's second year.

Gradually, I became aware of, if not capable of, the kind of selfless love demanded by parenthood and did not confuse it any longer with the pastel sentiments and self-satisfactions of caring for babies. I tried to jolt myself into realizing that each new conception meant only two years at most of accommodating babyhood, followed by a lifetime with a distinct personality to be loved for no other reason than its origin from God.

All these circumstances combined to end our "honeymoon" with parenthood. When my cycle returned after the second weaning, I was quite determined that surely we would now take every precaution within rhythm and not conceive again. I had considered everything but the state of my husband's emotions. The conditions prevailing in his first job were frustrating and tense. In my little-discussed assumption that we should now allow the maximum safety of an eight- or ten-day abstinence, he felt similarly frustrated and felt me in the controlling position. I think he found himself almost on purpose ignoring my desire for absolute safety. Obviously, my nonsexual behavior at the time did not provide him any comfort in reducing his conflicts. What my failing was I can't remember, but I know that the conflict about the children which I have described, as well as my effort to complete work for my degree, was leaving me little energy to consider Kenny's needs. I stopped my resistance to what I knew was dangerous timing of intercourse just short of refusal, as I had to, and our third child was conceived.

The malignant resentment which then began to take over my soul was soon mercifully relieved by three circumstances: our meetings with an excellent spiritual advisor, the completion of my master's degree, and a change of environment when Kenny took a new teaching job. By the time our little girl was born the immediate arguments we had held against her conception had vanished, and her sex made her additionally welcome. We have managed, not exactly easily, but willingly.

But the general reasons for limiting our family remain. My ability to truly love my children is increasing only slowly. The care required for another baby would sadly limit the attention and supervision I could give to the older children, who really need it to nourish their awakening personalities. There is nothing extraordinary about this in our present situation, but another baby would paralyze my physical mobility for the boys' entire preschool period. If their father were in a less demanding profession it might not be so important. As a Ph.D. candidate and full-time teacher he has no free time, nor does he expect to have much more when the time presently spent on his dissertation will be replaced by the research which is now a necessity in the teaching profession.

None of these facts seems cogent compared to the often-evoked picture of the heroic Catholic family of eight or more fighting all the odds which society can present, but we feel that there must be "many mansions" within the sacrament of marriage. Surely preparation and personality justify individual patterns determined not only by the forces of individual fertility. We know now that our dreams of a large family were sentimental. The fact that I learned nothing about the practical virtues of motherhood from my own home, and that I actually rejected everything relating to motherhood until I could intellectually appreciate the sacrament of marriage have something to do with the number of children I should be prepared to raise. My recent good will toward the sacrament did not change my abilities. Only truly extraordinary grace, on which I have no right to depend, could make me a good mother of a large family. On the other hand, my real education was for a nonfeminine type of intellectual activity, for which I have been extensively and expensively educated. I may not have been particularly worthy of this education, but it is a fact, and I believe that I can serve society through it. Having a large family would certainly frustrate this possibility, whereas its realization will not eventually harm, and probably will actually enrich, my present children. Working out such a balance of activity would itself be part of my vocation and would call upon most of my faculties.

The possibility of using periodic abstinence to limit our family from now on has finally become real. This possibility is the fruit both of self-sacrifice and of chance, and it appears providential to us. After our third baby was weaned (purposely earlier than the others) Kenny, independently of me, decided on complete continence until the reappearance of menstruation, a period of about two months. I was overjoyed by the spontaneity of his decision, which has marked a change in his willingness for control since then. We had a few occasions of intercourse during the month of the first period as the cycle and our work schedules allowed before the children and I left Kenny to spend the entire summer in the West at my parents' invitation. This separation had surface justifications (that is, collecting money for a house down-payment), but its principal purpose for us was the undisturbed operation of my menstrual cycle for three months while I charted temperature data. Such an opportunity for separation at such a vital time gave us invaluable ground for resuming our sexual relations safely. Our reading of J.G.H. Holt's *Marriage and Periodic Abstinence*, the first book we had found which stressed all the considerations necessary for absolute safety within rhythm, has helped us to a so far unshaken determination to allow no temporal possibility of conception. We now interrupt intercourse from the seventeenth day from my shortest known period (that is, the tenth day) until after the third consecutive morning of recorded high temperature, according to instructions in Holt's book. This has amounted to an abstinence of nine days. Taking temperature properly is hindered by the extreme wakefulness of the children; so that we must sometimes rely on counting days anyway.

If this system, now easily followed for four months, should fail, there would be no providential separation to help us out after the birth. A fourth child could be taken in stride, but the likelihood of further conceptions during the uncertain postpartum would gravely concern us. The only course open would be complete abstinence for the better part of a year until the cycle had operated several months. Waiting until the first month of operation would be risky because the cycle takes several months to resume its stable length. And, undoubtedly, abstinence is easier in separation.

If the system of periodic abstinence were the only restraint in our love-making, it could be much more easily tolerated. Although its strictures are the most inescapable, the others which come from the daily circumstances of this period of our life restrict spontaneity just as heavily.

Since we never have been free of really pressing professional obligations, we have never experienced any considerable period of relaxation to which we could compare the present status quo. In most cases, the only "adjustment" that ever concerns us is the choice of a time less disadvantageous than another—for instance, when only one of us is tired. Fatigue (mostly mine) and work (mostly Kenneth's) and the wakefulness of children (this has become a standard joke with us since it has happened so often) consistently discourage the frequency of our intercourse. While we had only one baby, it was our habit to have a certain subtle though unverbalized awareness of the imminence of intercourse, which allowed us mutually to plan a reasonable period of leisure to prepare for the occasion. Except for very rare occasions now, this fortunate and all but necessary preparation has disappeared. Kenneth's ever present work, and his inclination for working at night, makes the normal bedtime hour his most productive working period, and with several children other times for intercourse are quite impossible.

Since the arrival of our second child and most emphatically since our third, my 7 a.m. to 10 p.m. working day, with no possibility for naps, makes me extremely sleepy as soon as my activity stops, if not before. During our first two years or so I occasionally took pleasure in initiating love-making myself. I don't even consider it now, when my only feeling is that I had better save all my energy for those occasions when Kenneth is sufficiently interested to break his work. Then, I am likely to fight sleepiness during the entire act, and it is the truth, I think, to say that I am relieved when I can finally sleep. During recent months when the work schedule has been heaviest, the combination of restraints has reduced our relations during the safe period (which had been usually two a week); so that the safe period tends to slip by unused, and then, suddenly, the nine- or ten-day period of abstinence is upon us without our having made up for it previously.

I mention these kinds of deterrents, knowing that they are

trivial compared to the kinds of tragic frustrations which afflict
some marriages, but I mention them because of the light they
bring to the context in which sexual problems are discussed by
some of the best Catholic authors, that is, the control-release
dichotomy. Discussion of the problems of rhythm often con-
cludes with a statement to the effect that, after all is said and
done, the real problem remains: that of spiritual control of
concupiscence, rather than that of birth regulation.* I have
great regard for this generalization, when it can be made. As
my descriptions illustrate, our daily schedule simply crowds out
concupiscence to the degree that it needs very little spiritual
attention. We have so little opportunity to avail ourselves of
the welfare that harmonious sexual union can offer!

If physical satisfaction could be separated from psychological
and spiritual benefits, we could place more value on abstinence.
Instead, sexual union seems to be the most powerful means
at our disposal of putting to death the selfish and evil urges
we feel when our impaired natures are too much strained in
their task of commitment to complete self-giving. The most
marked complaint I have found in our long abstinences has
been the preoccupation of my consciousness with continual
petty complaints and resentments. And it is not (rather un-
happily, as I am about to explain) that the physical delight
rendered by my mate normally makes up for these sore spots;
it is rather that intercourse is a persuasive symbol of selflessness,
and a real refreshment of charity even when it occurs under
distracting circumstances. At times when I am really in need
of its healing, it is the uncharity already at work in my soul
which specifically resists the prospect of intercourse.

I will conclude by describing my response to prolonged abstinence, and in doing so I will have to describe conditions
which would cause disciples of the modern emphasis on "adjustment" to despair entirely of harmony in our marriage. I
leave it until last because I am certain that its importance is

* I am thinking of Marc Oraison, *Man and Wife.*

not supreme and that it need not color everything I have said. I am one of those women whose capacity for the sensual dynamics of intercourse has somehow been damaged. "Damaged" is the correct word in my case, because up until the very day of marriage my sexual responses, repressed as they were then, seemed to me extremely strong. Even now they are not nonexistent because I do experience them in dreams, and I can be easily aroused by the general subject of sex. Whatever has happened perplexes me totally and depresses me seriously if I concentrate upon the loss of something that seems as vital, in marriage, as any one of the five senses. Obviously my emotions in intercourse could not remain untouched by this circumstance, but I am thankful that they are not negatively affected. Whatever its explanation, this state of affairs drastically affects the spiritual implications of both abstinence and intercourse. It means that my principal satisfaction is the emotional-spiritual re-creation I have described; this is, therefore, the only thing I have to lose in abstinence. Abstinence, as a result, cannot ever serve me as a spiritual exercise in control and mortification. In fact, it is more likely to guarantee my sensual satisfaction in badly needed sleep. When my husband did undertake abstinence partially as a spiritual exercise one Lent, I was unable to join him. My only contribution could be more attention to the charity of my daily life with him to ease his difficulties.

My response to periodic abstinence is ambivalent. On one hand, the interval of abstinence stimulates at least my emotional anticipation. On the other hand, I can come closest to sensual involvement when there is special preparation or when there is a special occasion of mutual recreation or emotional importance. Clearly, the choice of occasions by the calendar, not to mention the other limitations upon us, reduces this kind of opportunity to a minimum. If cases like mine are actually as common as reports indicate, any emphasis on concupiscence in the question of sex in marriage is irrelevant.

Mr. H continues the witness:

I am writing separately from my wife because the nature of my commitment to marriage is different from hers. Perhaps any man's is different from any woman's, but the danger of this kind of writing is that one is inclined to generalize on the basis of his own situation, and I do not want to do this any more than I want to imply that my situation is unique. At any rate, I am committed to marriage by the same act in which I am committed to life itself. If this sounds either self-evident or hammy in my way of putting it, it is not so in fact. The same qualities of intellectual curiosity, of desire to understand and to give understanding, of delight in the manifestation of God's presence in the world, and of hilarity at the graces with which we clothe our absurdities to call them communication, these same qualities that led to my decision to be a teacher-scholar are manifested in my attitude toward my marriage. They are a part of me, or a part of that part of me that I can understand, and I don't feel that estrangement between myself as a professional man and myself as a husband that I have observed in others. But if this solves some problems, it only causes others. If there is some conflict between my work and my marriage rooted in my personality, there is also conflict in the demands they each make on me in the temporal order.

Scholarship demands as much as one can give it, and often I find it necessary to deny myself to my family because of my profession. The problem of adjusting to the specific demands of each would be easy if I could continually dismiss one in favor of the other, but this kind of preference is impossible. It is about as unlikely that I should change my profession as it is that I should get divorced (and perhaps in some ways as immoral), and simply being a responsible member of that profession involves a series of demands which conflict with those of my family at given moments of time. Thus the problem resolves itself into a number of prudential decisions in specific cases: I am working well on a train of thought that could be valuable; shall I stay up late to see what I can make of it and ask my wife to wake me late tomorrow, even though it will complicate her life because tomorrow is her day for the car-pool? She wants to spend the evening discussing whether we can afford to send our eldest son to a private kindergarten next year, and if we can afford it, whether it would be worthwhile. Can I prepare my class in the one hour I have tomorrow, rather than the three I have tonight? The focus of my life depends on the answers to a continuing series of nagging, minor questions like these, and there is no escape from the tedium of devoting no small portion of my energies to such decisions. This problem is by no means eased by the fact that we have three preschool children.

For one thing, I find lecturing to large sections an exhausting task and am often very tired when I come home with more work for the evening. At the same time, my wife has become worn out by the constant attention which three young children demand. It is easy for both of us to become selfish and to prefer our own needs to those of the family. Dinner is often a strain, and since the children, despite all efforts, seldom go to bed early, it is usually nine or later before I can tackle the paper corrections, the class preparation, or the work on my dissertation which I must accomplish before going to bed. I have to fight through family annoyances, I feel, in order to fulfill my obligations as a teacher and, on the other hand, I must fight through a pile of work in order to spend any time with my family. Thus, although there is a basic unity in my role as father in a family and my fatherlike role as a teacher and scholar, this unity is all too seldom realized in actual fact.

It is not hard to recognize that in such a situation it is difficult for me to have a meaningful sexual relationship with my wife. Probably in part because of one parent's selfish and destructive attitude toward sex, and in part because of the insecurities of her own early sexual experience, she is not a person whose physical responses are very immediate or very strong. Most of her joy in the sexual act is emotional. Because of faults of personality in both of us, she receives little physical satisfaction in intercourse. The prognosis should be good, however. Despite our faults we love each other deeply and are aware of the problems that interfere with our achieving sexual harmony. In the passing of time, as our maturity and understanding increase, our life together will take on that unity in love which sexuality reflects. This is how our progress should be, but the likelihood of that progress is remote. Because so much of our lives is caught in the tension between our individual selves and the sacramental self (the sanctifying of body and spirit through the mutual exchange that is rooted in sexuality), we cannot nurture our love until the pressures that now take all our mental and spiritual energies are released.

Looming large among those pressures is the rhythm method. I should be wrong were I to say, as I am tempted to, that we could not afford more children financially. We cannot afford them emotionally and spiritually. I cannot permit my wife's inherent talent and basic good will to be destroyed by promiscuous breeding. Even the children we now have, especially the younger boy, are threatened not by lack of love but by lack of attention. Until the birth of our last child, I had visions of an open-ended family with an indefinite number of children to come, perhaps, when the children we now have grow old enough to be less demanding. I now want no more children, ever. Sending them to college will pose a grave financial crisis for me, but more than that, I wish my wife to be freed from the burdens of raising children. I want her to be able to enrich the family and to contribute to society by resuming the activities for which she was trained. (She turned down the opportunity for a large fellowship, which would have enabled her to continue graduate work, because of her responsibility as a mother.) I am tired of the old bromide that the woman's role is in the home. I married my wife as a person, not as a role!

While the marriage and the children who have come from it have imposed burdens which she has willingly accepted, she cannot continue to do so unless she can look to something beyond the frustrations which three very active children bring. I know many women who, in their early forties, have begun a rich and meaningful new life after their children have become self-sufficient. My wife has the aptitudes for a full, rich motherhood, made fuller and richer by being combined with other activities. Thus, so that we could love our children better by not mixing our love with the bitterness of sacrificing our own needs to them, we have decided to have no more children.

But here the problem arises. My wife has fifteen to twenty childbearing years ahead of her. We have strong and, I think, justified reasons for having no more children. The only way in which we can prevent conception is rhythm. But to be completely effective this means we must abstain from intercourse for almost half of the menstrual cycle. Thus we cannot make any significant progress on achieving a more satisfactory sexual relationship, because we are bound by her body temperature rather than by the nature of our love-relationship at a particular time, by our desire to communicate in this way, and by our emotional needs. This is the situation that faces us for the next twenty years, unless we should choose to do incalculable harm to ourselves and our present children by raising more children than we are emotionally suited to raise or, on the other hand, decide to use some other method of birth control.

This last alternative I rule out categorically, but not because I believe that other forms of birth control are immoral. On the contrary I believe they are moral, and although I would reject most methods for aesthetic reasons, I would be quite willing to practice birth control through the new pills. The reason for our not practicing this form of birth control is that I feel no moral scruples impelling me to do so, and in the absence of moral scruples of private conscience, I follow the Church's teachings as an act of obedience. The whole situation is not very satisfactory, but my wife and I try to make it something valuable through our knowledge that our self-sacrifice is the result of our love for each other, and through our faith that this self-sacrifice is a means to our sanctification.

Our marriage is not, perhaps, as hopeless as it sometimes seems when I reflect upon its negative aspects—and I have by no means covered all these aspects here. Because of our own imperfections, perfection in marriage is impossible. Because of our own imperfections and the constraining situation in which we must try to cope with them, complete satisfaction in marriage seems impossible. But because of God's grace, because of our unity in love, and because of the basic stability of our personalities, we are ultimately happy and our marriage is basically good. We must continually try to unite in that happiness and to make that goodness into joy.

CHAPTER NINE

A Failure

in Education

Mr. and Mrs. I have now been married three years and have two children. They have lived briefly abroad, but now are living in an Eastern city.

Mrs. I writes:

Several serious problems face those who attempt to live a Catholic marriage in our society. Many of the difficulties grow out of the confused attitude toward sex prevalent in American Catholic life.

The Catholic entering marriage with a thorough Catholic education, it seems to us, is poorly prepared for the reality of marriage. My husband and I attended Catholic grade schools, high schools, and colleges. Our education included several courses on "Christian Marriage," extensive reading about Catholic marriage—from classroom pamphlets about "The Right Partner for You!" to books given to us by our parents on "Sex in God's Plan." Before we were married we had read the popes, the fathers of the Church, St. Paul, and scores of popular Catholic writers on sex and marriage. We attended career-day lectures on marriage and followed Catholic discussions about the need for sacrifice by husband and wife. Our background was completely Catholic: we grew up in Catholic families where no one questioned the indissolubility of the marriage bond or other traditional Catholic views.

In all of these years of preparation, I don't remember the word intercourse ever being mentioned. I expected great revelations in a college course on marriage in which the male students took a separate course from the women. Instead, the priest droned on for a semester about the nature of the contract (it would have provided a good background if I had intended to be a canon lawyer; it was a waste of time as a background for marriage). One day a doctor came in to give us the "real facts." I can't remember anything he said; I suspect he said nothing to disturb my ignorance. My husband's education included similar useless courses.

I grew up with a naïve distorted attitude toward sex, which I picked up from reading the pious Catholic literature on the subject, and from passively accepting the nonsense taught by a few neurotic nuns and priests. I remember one nun who told us in high school that when a boy wanted to kiss us we should hold up a picture of the Blessed Virgin and let him kiss that instead! To an adult, the advice is ludicrous; to a confused adolescent, schooled in obedience to the religious, attitudes like these only throw the developing conscience into deeper disorder.

We were often warned about getting our knowledge of sex "from the gutter." Perhaps I would have been much healthier—spiritually and psychologically—had I read some of the cheap literature available on the subject. My husband read medical books on sex which his parents gave to him. His understanding of sex was superior to mine.

Sex should have been discussed frankly with us by our parents. It wasn't. Their tensions and reluctance to discuss the experience of marriage left a vacuum that could not be filled by classes, books, or conversations with friends.

My ignorance was not the "beautiful innocence" which Catholic vigilantes warn us not to lose. It was an ugly distortion in which the role of sex had been shoved aside, replaced by layers of sentimental drivel. Had someone told me that sex was wonderful, one of the greatest experiences of life, I would have been shocked. Sex was wrong before marriage, and a sacred duty afterward—"the Catholic approach" had given me the guiding principles.

Many of my friends responded to their Catholic education about sex by rejecting "the Catholic approach" as unrealistic. They formed a conscience influenced by prevailing opinions on good and evil. For them, hours in lovers' lanes were good—an indication of popularity; getting pregnant before marriage was bad. Some of the same cynicism probably now helps them decide questions like birth control.

I held onto "the Catholic approach," faithful that my idealism would lead to the conjugal joy pictured in the pamphlets and textbooks. It nearly led me to disaster.

Had I not fallen in love with a non-Catholic and been forced by the reality of love to question my blind faith, I might still be in a state of "blessed singleness" (as they call it in the pamphlets), embittered with frustration. Fortunately, my non-Catholic romance did not work out, but it did jar my passive acceptance of "the Catholic approach." When I did meet the Catholic man I married, I still had years of distortion to overcome; I expect shadows of it will remain with me the rest of my life.

Courtship proved one of the most difficult periods of my life: balancing an uncertain conscience against the reality of love left me with painful soul-searching and frequent trips to the confessional—which often only added to the confusion. When we decided to marry, I realized I was entering a state which I had

read about but hardly understood. I knew I was marrying a
religious man, who could help me meet the confusion without
shattering the religious base of my ideals. With the help of the
sacrament of matrimony, prayer, and the Mass, I hoped that our
love would grow into a healthy marriage. Sexual union, like
childbirth, is almost impossible to understand before it is experienced. Because I knew so little about sex, I didn't worry that
it would offer many problems.

In the first weeks of marriage, I was able to discuss moral
qualms with a sympathetic confessor. His attitude—so open
to the power of love—greatly helped me to answer the moral
questions that suddenly appeared when married sexual life
began. One of the most burdensome of these problems was
whether it is immoral to reach a climax outside of intercourse
at the beginning of marriage, when even preliminary exchanges
of love are stimulating to that level. As valuable as the confessor's guidance was, it should not have been necessary. Some-
where in our background these questions should have been
answered, or at least discussed. I should have approached marriage as secure in my moral outlook as in my love.

Years of married life may be required before some areas of
sexual adjustment are worked out in a pattern satisfactory to
husband and wife. Reaching a coordinated climax, or even,
for the wife, reaching a climax in the act of intercourse, may
be difficult. Such problems can only be resolved with love and
patience between husband and wife. So many tensions interfere with modern life that even relaxation in love takes effort;
besides this, the years of sexual taboos may take years of
married sexual life to overcome.

If the couple is not practicing rhythm and can have intercourse frequently, when their emotions require it, many daily
strains of married life seem to take care of themselves. Frequent intercourse not only builds a happy sexual life, but can
also lead to a happier mental and spiritual life since these are
one for the married couple. Sexual life is not an independent

part of daily living, which can be used or neglected like liquor or cigarettes. It *is* daily living. Psychologists have pointed out this relationship for years, and our experience verifies it.

The moral questions about sex in marriage gradually shift from problems like that of reaching a climax in intercourse to the more uncertain area of intercourse for procreation and pleasure.

Since pregnancy followed soon after marriage for us, the question of rhythm and birth control didn't become significant until after the birth of the first child. We had no desire to limit our family at the beginning of married life—we could enjoy sexual life without the worry of "ovulation periods" and other considerations in the practice of rhythm. We think rhythm imposes many strains on a couple: the first months of married life offer enough challenges in adjustment without the added burden of rhythm.

Childbirth was a beautiful experience, which added a deeper spiritual dimension to our sexual life. When a theology of sex is developed, we hope it will delve into the spiritual relationship of the act of childbirth to the act of intercourse. Beyond their obvious tie is a deeper relationship which has not been fully explored. A conscious childbirth brings with it many of the same physical and mental sensations as intercourse—to a much heightened degree; the final expulsion of the child is an overwhelming climax, taking a woman to the height of exhilaration and then exhaustion. One contrast between childbirth and intercourse is the source of stimulation, which is not directly the husband but the child. Sexual life has then expanded from the husband-wife relationship to the husband-wife-child in a direct sensual pattern.

Childbirth can be an almost mystical experience, in which discomfort and pleasure, fatigue and exhilaration merge with an acute spiritual awareness, temporarily elevating a woman from the ordinary plane of life. I have felt my creative energy to be at its peak at the time of childbirth, and for several hours afterward. My perception is sharper, my sensitivity and observation of life around me deeper than at most other times in my life. Where is God in this experience? Christ? the Mystical Body?

It is disappointing to me that I have no real feeling of God's presence at the time of childbirth, little urge to pray, no sense of unity with humanity. I would think all of these thoughts should enter the mind of a woman bringing new life into the world. But they appear in the conscience much later. At childbirth, I noticed particularly the pettiness of man in the face of life's overwhelming experiences, like the exchange of sarcasm between two nurses when one walked out just before delivery. Perhaps such things are more noticeable because a woman is briefly lifted above them at childbirth. Could there be a spiritual preparation for childbirth during pregnancy, just as there are physical exercises for childbirth? How can a woman relate to God during labor—formula prayers are even more of a strain than in ordinary circumstances, and meditation is blurred by physical and mental stress.

We do not think that Catholics have touched the surface of these questions. In some cities, Catholic hospital staffs are so opposed to natural childbirth that a women must go to a non-Catholic hospital if she wants support in her desire for the conscious experience of childbirth. The only hospitals in some American cities teaching methods of natural childbirth, methods encouraged by the popes, are Protestant and Jewish. Naturally, nothing significant can be developed on the relation of childbirth to the spiritual life if women sleep through the experience.

As is well known among psychologists—and often ignored among Catholics—the exhilaration of childbirth fades quickly. After the birth of the first baby (and perhaps after each one), the mother may experience not only post-partum despondency but many other physical, mental, and spiritual anxieties related to being a mother. Unlike the stereotypes in Catholic publications, most women do not joyfully launch into motherhood waving their banners of sacrifice. Few women in our society are accustomed to the confinement that comes with a new baby; a woman who has led an active life suddenly finds her world reduced to diapers and worry about why the baby is crying. Often in Catholic discussions, we brush off post-partum depression as psychological distortion or the result of a selfish outlook. A Catholic woman may feel particularly confused by her mixed reactions to motherhood.

I have known few new mothers who escaped some depression after the baby was born. It may be only a slight loss of energy and interest in the outside world, which passes in a few weeks, or a deep withdrawal which lasts for years. Several friends have never returned to their former alertness after the birth of the first baby. Nature requires some slowing down after birth, so that the mother and infant will get the rest they need. Even the most happy mother with an ideal child will find herself somewhat on edge and fatigued.

Besides the mother's instability at this time, a crying baby enters the previously private life of the couple. Great joy also enters into the marriage as the couple watches the result of their love develop into an independent human being. But the total view is not as carefree as many Catholic writers paint it. A Catholic couple adds the strain of rhythm after the birth of the baby (unless they want a child every nine months). The woman's anxiety can become worse as the artificial sexual life introduced with rhythm interferes with natural impulses, setting up acute psychological stress.

We faced another problem at this time, which must trouble many Catholic couples. If the woman nurses the baby, her menstruation period probably will be completely irregular or she may not menstruate at all. How is the couple to practice rhythm? Non-Catholic doctors advise some other form of birth control during this time. They point out that women often don't get pregnant while they nurse a baby, but there is no certainty about it. If a Catholic couple rejects artificial contraception, what alternatives do they have? Complete abstinence from sexual intercourse while the baby is being nursed—which may be as long as a year—places an almost unbearable burden on the couple.

Many Catholic mothers say the risk of a second pregnancy following immediately is not balanced by the unknown benefits of nursing. But a Catholic couple may feel, as we did, that the value of nursing the baby is so great it justifies upsetting the rhythm schedule.

If there were more frank discussions among married Catholics, problems like these could be clarified. Someone may have found a solution which would help others facing the same thing. Even conversations among married couples which go beyond grudging acceptance of Church discipline are rare. A friend says she wishes more Catholic women, especially, would discuss sexual life, but she can find hardly any who will talk about it. The most common talk of sex we have heard among married Catholics revolves around off-color jokes. In general, our contacts with the clergy have not helped us, either.

When I asked a confessor (not the same one as in the beginning of marriage) about using rhythm for a few months after I stopped nursing the baby, I was dismayed by his attitude: as if the idea of a mother with one child wanting to use rhythm was selfish. His fears were unnecessary: rhythm is haphazard for many women, and a second pregnancy soon followed for us.

Why does the clergy take such an unsympathetic view of the problems facing parents? Probably because they are not married. They do not meet the chaos of several children crammed into an overcrowded apartment—many American cities are not geared to large families and it is impossible to find adequate space at a reasonable rent. Nor do they pay a $500 hospital and delivery bill. Many health insurance plans, we find, are not designed for large families; in some states the most common plans pay about 15 percent of the total bill. Parish priests usually are overworked, but they do not have the added burden of maintaining some peace of mind in the middle of the incessant demands of children. I've found it difficult simply to continue a healthy spiritual life, for I cannot get to frequent Mass and reception of the sacraments now while the small children cannot be left alone. Perhaps religious base many of their ideas of family life on memories of their families, in which they lived as children, not as adults who had to worry about the problems. The responsibilities of parenthood must be lived to be fully understood.

Our short experience in trying to live a Catholic marriage leads us to a few hopes for changes in the Church's approach. We hope the Church will reexamine its attitude on Catholic marriage, especially birth control. We hear a whimper of change here and there, but not the uproar needed to end outmoded approaches. We would like to see the Church begin a worldwide program of responsible parenthood. Begetting children should be a conscious act, freely willed by both parents, not an animal process beyond their control. Can Catholics emphasize free will in all areas of moral behavior, then deny its role in the greatest human act—bringing new life into the world?

A woman is fertile for a relatively short time in each month and she is "in heat" after her period of ovulation. This suggests that nature has not designed her for repeated pregnancies—it is more natural not to be having children than to have them. She is most eager for intercourse when she is least likely to become pregnant. Can we continue to insist that natural law forbids contraception when nature provides strong natural barriers to conception?

Continence at times probably leads to greater love in sexual union. But the kind of continence demanded by rhythm (in its present uncertainty) seems to us morally questionable over a long period of time. Love cannot be turned on like a faucet at certain times of the month and shut off during fertile periods. This "natural" form of birth control may be the most unnatural method. A Catholic mother with three small children told us recently that the Church's position on rhythm ought to be reversed. The Church allows rhythm for a serious reason, only as long as the reason continues, and so on. . . . Instead, the Church ought to allow children only for serious reasons.

Unless the Church changes its outlook toward birth control—so that it explores and advocates every moral form of birth regulation—we fear increased acceptance of an ugly nonreligious approach to the creation of life. We notice how strongly Americans protest that their tax dollars are being wasted in underdeveloped countries where birth control does not limit the hungry mouths of the poor. We see the expanding sympathy for sterilization of overproductive welfare cases. These attitudes, though coldly realistic, repel the people of countries unaccustomed to an American's impersonal, efficient way of thinking.

Should we be surprised that the solutions proposed are anti-Christian when the Church has turned away from any suggestion of birth control? As soon as someone advances an idea on birth control, we expect to see the local hierarchy slapping back with its official condemnation. Yet the people who advance it often are deeply religious men and women searching for moral answers.

After living in underdeveloped countries for a while, we disagree with some of the hysterical theory on the population explosion—in many countries we have seen, the problem is not as much overpopulation as underdevelopment of existing resources, land, and people. In some underdeveloped countries where we lived and visited, having children is one of the few joys left to the poor. The rich, backed by the silence of the Church, have deprived them of most other forms of human satisfaction.

At the same time, we have talked with priests in underdeveloped countries who question how morally responsible human beings can be when they grow up in a family of ten or more, crowded into one room. The sexual perversions which result ought to goad hesitant Catholics into more positive attitudes toward birth regulation. For the Church is the main hope for responsible parenthood in many parts of the world, especially Latin America. Unless the Church sets up birth regulation centers throughout the world, to teach birth regulation and to advance research, we think the immorality of the present situation will weigh even more heavily on the Catholic conscience.

A reexamination of traditional Catholic attitudes on birth control is as necessary within the American Catholic mentality as it is in underdeveloped countries. We allow the production-line heresy to twist our ideas on marriage: the Catholic family of the year is the family of eleven. We hear Catholic parents speak of their children in terms of numbers—"our number six," "we're expecting our seventh" (followed by a big laugh).

One primary purpose of marriage is the procreation *and education* of offspring. In the papal writing we have read on the subject, these two points are joined. But in the United States we frequently forget the last half. When anyone emphasizes the responsibility to educate the children, some Catholics think he means only sending them to Catholic schools, while others take it to mean limiting the family to be able to afford sending them to expensive schools.

We think our responsibility to educate our children means the total development of each child (in the limited way any human can be helped to achieve his total possibilities). When the mother is too overworked to guide this individual development, the couple has not only the right but the obligation to limit its family. Some couples can have ten children and give each the love it needs for its healthy growth. Others are overwhelmed with one. This is a question each couple must decide. A confessor may give good advice, but the moral obligation of deciding the family's limits—or perhaps the parents' limitations—should rest with the couple.

Needless to say, problems like these depend on complete agreement between husband and wife. Compromise may be worked out in other areas of married life—financial responsibility, daily living problems—but sexual life allows few compromises. If the wife feels overburdened but compromises her wishes for a small family, in order to meet her husband's desire not to practice rhythm, she will be unhappy no matter how strong her willingness to sacrifice. If the husband compromises his need for a healthy sexual life to his wife's wishes not to have children he also will be frustrated. These tensions lead to many unhappy marriages, perhaps contributing to neurosis and mental illness.

Another area needing reexamination is the couple's personal development in marriage. Man and wife need to continue their individual and mutual development as the family grows. Many Catholics, however, believe that other interests should automatically become secondary to the children, an attitude that leads to spoiled, overprotected children and dull parents unable to talk about anything more exciting than the latest case of diaper rash. We are surprised how many priests, especially, expect that a woman will naturally drop her interest in personal development for the sake of her family. Perhaps they base their attitudes on sentimental portraits of their mothers. This is unrealistic, even un-Christian. Each individual human has the right to the complete development of his intellectual, physical, spiritual abilities—as Pope John said in *Pacem in Terris*. We find a contrast between Pope John's attitude toward women's rights, as reflected in the encyclical, and that in many magazines and sermons.

A woman who cuts off her abilities beyond bringing up a family wastes potential given her by God. Motherhood may be her greatest ability (though that is questionable), but she is not a machine designed to keep the human race in existence. She is a free human being with responsibilities in developing a sensitive social conscience and contributing to the life of art, culture, politics.

Childbirth does not fully satisfy a woman's creative desires. It completes the act of love; it cannot replace other creative achievement. Writing a book is not at all like giving birth to a child; it is nonsense to say women do not write or paint because they have children. Often they are too lazy to discipline themselves for creative work, or else too overworked. In the case of Catholic women, there is little incentive for intellectual achievement in their backgrounds, and they have been warned since grade school not to "let their careers stand in the way of their families." (How many follow careers which could stand in the way?) A woman's career naturally will be somewhat slowed by a growing family—how much so depends partly on her ability to organize her work and use her time well.

My husband and I have less time to waste than before our children were born, but we hope our intellectual growth has not been stunted because of them. So far, both of us have been able to continue our education and our careers with our family. We hope our children can grow up without the distorted Catholic attitudes we faced. If the general Catholic attitude toward sex is to change, the attitudes of teaching priests and nuns, as well as parents, must change. Married laymen with a healthy outlook ought to assume a greater role in sex education, including teaching and writing the Catholic books and pamphlets on marriage.

We remember how often in books and classrooms the Church's teaching on the problem of the mother's life versus the child's was discussed. The approach was a brutal application of principle which frightened many girls. This problem is so rare that we wonder why it is mentioned at all. Yet it often occupies a place in Catholic marriage courses, along with stress on how wrong sexual relations are before marriage; why birth control, abortion, divorce, and polygamy are wrong.

We doubt that married laymen would emphasize this negative, legalistic approach.

Poor sex education harms many besides married couples. It leads to lonely Catholic women who could have married had they not been brought up with a rigid fear of sex. We know many unhappy Catholic girls whose sexual backgrounds have been distorted to the point of permanent psychological damage by the confused attitudes toward sex we have described. We also know effeminate Catholic men—intelligent, conscientiously Catholic, and damaged for life. Both problems seem to us widespread.

American Catholics are not alone in the confusion. But we have observed a much healthier attitude toward sex among Catholics of other countries.

In this discussion, we have stressed problems which can face a Catholic couple, because many of these areas are seldom mentioned. We should not want to give the impression that a Catholic marriage is one overwhelming difficulty piled on another. Nor do we question the Catholic position on many of these problems as much as the general Catholic attitude toward them. But when the Church reexplores its thinking on the experience of Catholic marriage, we hope it will seek leadership from the lay people who are living it.

Mr. I adds:

My major anxiety as a married man has been, after sixteen years of Catholic schooling, my inadequate preparation for marriage. Two years in a novitiate allow one to test cloistered life, but I know of no Catholic *School for Husbands.* How such studied ignorance can persist about married love, which St. Paul compared to Christ's love for His Church, still baffles me.

Most of the classes and sermons on sex which I suffered through prior to my marriage stressed the fact that sexual activity belongs to marriage. They had put such distorted emphasis on the sexual activity not permitted before marriage, however, that they ruptured the continuity in the whole process of love. From a state of fear about our natural passions preceding marriage, we were supposed to enter the freedom of holy matrimony. We were somehow supposed to be enriched in our later capacity to love, by our prior vigilance.

How unrealistic this appears when considered against the confusion and failures accompanying our early attempts to consummate our marriage. It may seem humorous now, but from no point of view did our awkwardness exemplify a new freedom. Instead, it suggested the continuation of an instilled fear, guilt, and repulsion about sexual activity. We did not know how much we had to learn. None of the medical books I had read discussed the difficulties of learning to love well; different positions were listed as casually as physical conditioning exercises. For a while the sexual intercourse I had expected to be the natural fruition of our love was as complicated as a new household gadget which defied mastery.

I have come to believe that marital sex problems arise as soon as one isolates coitus from the whole continuum of conjugal activities. To me expressions such as "the *use* of intercourse" and "*making* love" treat sexual activity as another expendable commodity. I find the concepts of indulgence and self-control just as materialistic. Fasting from food is ordinarily used as an analogy with abstention from coitus. But my own experience has been that temperament, fatigue, and the weather are more relevant to the frequency of expressing marital love than the concepts of indulgence and self-control. Indulgence and self-control bring vices to my mind, the capital sins, not love nor a sacramental act.

During the first two years of our marriage, rhythm as such was never seriously practiced. Now that we have had two children in quick succession it will be necessary to practice rhythm until we can fully discharge our present responsibilities. There is nothing natural about the practice to me. To live by a lunar calendar with someone you love is more like a sanctioned occasion of sin. To say that we avoid interfering with natural functions by using rhythm seems to me to be nonsense. It would be more logical for me to reason that since my wife is more excitable physically and psychologically after ovulation, the primary function of coitus is not reproduction. If reproduction were the natural or primary function of coitus she should be more excitable just before ovulation or during it. The view that reproduction is the natural outcome of intercourse is contradicted by the fact that there are only forty-eight hours when conception is likely in the average twenty-eight day cycle. This means that the probability of conceiving is .07. This is hardly an overwhelming argument for the assumption that reproduction is the primary or natural end of intercourse.

Coordination in climax has been difficult to achieve. My principal concern about this has been the extent to which poor guidance and misdirection have contributed to our difficulties. I am concerned because it raises the question of how incomplete our education has been in other areas. As the ones responsible for the education of our children, I fail to see how we can send our children through school systems that allow them to be as confused in their attempts to love as we recognize ourselves to be.

My marriage has taught me how foolish it is to separate the rest of married life from sexual activity. In general, the quality of our sexual activity, that is, of all expressions of affection, reflects the harmony of our marriage at that time. Rhythm violates this harmony on the assumption that the desire for intercourse is as subject to the calendar as the buying of fish on Fridays.

Our conjugal relationship has brought into question the teaching function of the Church today. Without ignoring the instances in which Christ gave the Church authority to teach, it is impossible for me to avoid thinking that members of the Church have abused this authority when speaking of marriage. The existing emphasis on the law reminds me of Saul self-righteously persecuting Christians. I am sure that those who officiate so solemnly on the conduct of premarital and marital love would have pontificated in the same way at Cana. On hearing that the wine had run out they would have spoken of indulgence and self-control, of the necessity to curb our appetites, and with the academic detachment belying any pertinent experience they would have praised God for protecting the guests from excesses.

Christ made more wine. If our trademark as Christians is to be love, it will have to be given the freedom to grow in the family. Love does not resemble a legal process. I cannot separate the injustice and immorality that has reigned in so many Catholic countries from the failure to love in the most familiar, smallest circle, the family.

In the same manner I see a connection between our inadequacies and the attempt to model Christian marriage on the Holy Family. That marriage was nonconsummated; it was a contract entered into to give respectable parentage to the Messiah. The compulsive repetition of statements about Mary's virginity during her marriage is not a healthy preparation for marriage. The discomfort evidenced by married Catholics when they discuss sexual matters demonstrates how many still feel guilty, as if they had been naughty with their spouses. When I speak to married non-Catholics I enjoy the freedom from sniggers, blushes, and whispers which so often typifies Catholic discussion of sex. It distresses me to consider how much of this congenital sexual immaturity is bred from the Catholic pulpit and classroom.

Most of all, the exercise of sex in marriage has led me to question the relevance of Catholic instruction today. For example, laymen exposed to twenty-four college credits of philosophy in a Catholic college can spend months on the distinctions between legal and illegal abortions, but spend no time at all trying to understand and to criticize the many philosophies underlying the different child-rearing practices currently in vogue. The merit of such expensive instruction is questionable. Until Catholic discussion gives love and the psychology of marriage at least equal time with birth control, I do not see how anyone with a conscience can take it seriously.

CHAPTER TEN

It's in the Air

After fifteen years of marriage, Mr. and Mrs. J have four children. They live in the East, where Mr. J works for a newspaper.

Mr. J writes:

My wife and I look back over fifteen years of marriage and are astonished at how insignificant now seem the difficulties which youth and naïveté magnified into crises, and how blissfully innocent we were about the challenges of the wedded state. I suppose devout aunts ascribe to the working of Divine Providence (in answer, of course, to their fervent novenas) the happy union of two persons who had to contend with family reluctance to their marriage, ecclesiastical red tape of fantastic proportions, and worries of health and finance. But deep in our own hearts is the conviction that these external concerns, which in retrospect turned out to be quite minor, comprised the shield that protected us against the infinitely more urgent tensions of compatibility. We discovered that there is a terribly complex period during which two grow physically, emotionally, and intellectually into one, as, at the altar, with the sudden uttering of brief words, two became spiritually one.

We review that period (is it yet ended?) and the prospect of what might have been causes a shudder. Certainly innocence proved a blessing. But one wonders if under only slightly changed circumstances that same innocence might have been disastrous. I am not speaking here of the innocence of sexual experience, although that is a part of it. I am speaking more of innocence in understanding. We hardly knew what marriage meant, apart from the clipped definition which we learned out of the Baltimore Catechism years before. There is no manual of marriage, no matter how detailed, to which one can turn for instruction full and complete on the art of oneness, Christian or otherwise; nor will there ever be such a manual; nor should there be. But there is, or should be, a climate which in itself is educative, a climate which hints of the nature of marriage, which gives perspective to the effects of the sacrament, its duties and privileges.

As my wife and I reflect on the problems with which we were confronted in our adjustment to marriage, we are inclined to wonder if the greatest problem was not environmental, and whether many of those difficulties which were to plunge us into sullen moods and perplexing dilemmas did not arise out of the environment of our childhood and adolescence.

Our environment was no different, probably, than that of most Americans, certainly than that of most New England Catholics. Our parents were God-fearing people; they loved one another, and they loved and provided well for their children. Full praise be theirs. But for all the affection and the fun, there was a barrier. It was impossible to define this barrier clearly at the time. Now as we are older, with our own adult experience to draw upon, with children of our own and responsibilities kindred to those of our parents, we think we know the answer. We detect traces of Jansenism—the conflict of "supernatural" love versus "natural" love—in ourselves and in our relations with our children, and the thought immediately suggests itself that here is that barrier. We are sure of it. And as we look around us we ask if the barrier does not exist for Americans generally, particularly American Catholics.

Our observation is valid, we feel, despite the fact that side by side with the culture to which we attribute this Jansenist streak is a culture obsessed with sex—we see it in the books we read, our advertising, our entertainment media, and the fact that sexual license has never been greater in terms of divorce and premarital and extramarital adventures. If we were a Freudian analyst team we would argue that Americans are living in two worlds—a public world of eros and a private world of Jansenism —and that the two so clash as to make Americans the awkward and uncomfortable romantics which Europeans, with good cause, claim we are.

It would demand, admittedly, an extended dissertation to document this theory, and that is not our purpose. We raise the subject in order to demonstrate the particular difficulty which the conflict between inner instinct and external forces presented for us.

We feel as though we were, in a way, the victims of an unnatural combination of historical emphases with regard to sex and marriage. The national culture in which we find ourselves derives primarily from a Puritan past which so accented strictness in sexual discipline, which was so unbending and at times fanatic, that to enjoy even a wedding feast was regarded "as great a sin as for a Father to take a knife and cut his child's throat." Our culture has outgrown this form of extremism, but not before grains of joylessness and suspicion for the pleasure which under one circumstance is good and under another bad have rubbed off on us.

Happily, many Americans have never grown completely away from the importance which the Puritans attached to purity and the sanctity of marriage; but we are not blind to current divorce figures and various reports on the sex habits of American college students, suburban housewives, office secretaries, traveling salesmen, and others.

We note that when cases arise which seem to threaten traditional American virtues in a public way, Americans revert to character. Whatever their own personal habits and status, they react strongly against public flouting of these virtues. The morals of the country are not going to be influenced or corrupted by some light-headed movie stars or empty-headed athletes and playboys; we can follow the antics of this colony with tolerance, fascination, and amusement. When this same conduct crops up, however, in quarters to which we look for inspiration and leadership, a different standard entirely applies. The Puritan in us emerges and we become the stern judges our ancestors were in yesteryear.

There is hypocrisy perhaps in our tendency, but the tendency is there nonetheless. We might thrill to eros, but our instinct inclines us otherwise. We feel the conflict between the codes of conduct that American mores dictate to some, excuse in some, tolerate in some, and still demand in some.

Ideally one might expect us as Catholics to sail serenely over these waters troubled by Puritanism and indulgence. Our Church's position on marriage and the family is clear, constant, and uncompromising. It would seem that all we have to do is conform. But it is not so simple as all this. For one thing, we live in the same world as our neighbors, and it is unrealistic to tell us that we are going to be a part of this world without being touched by it. When we were married fifteen years ago, we were married with values conditioned by our secular environment; the conditioning may or may not be so pronounced as in the case of non-Catholics, but it does exist.

Moreover, additional complicating factors were introduced for us through the very teachings and traditions of our Church. If there were difficulties for us because of the clash between the Puritan and pagan values of our workaday world, they were less troublesome, really, than some of the conflicts for faith and conscience which we encountered in the sanctuary of Catholicism. The Church taught us a dichotomous approach to the heart of our marriage—our sexual relationship. The problem comes into focus as we examine the home and the spouses which the Church holds up as the models of Christian marital perfection—the Blessed Virgin and St. Joseph, the Holy Family of Nazareth.

It is a curious phenomenon that the Church which has done most to exalt the notion of family and preserve and safeguard its integrity is the same Church which, for better or worse, has interlarded its doctrine with beliefs which come close to distorting what it seeks to ennoble. The Holy Family is quite rightly the object of our prayers and our emulation. But the inspiration and lesson of the Holy Family is almost lost in one or two misplaced emphases. One of these surely is the emasculation of St. Joseph and the attributing to him of a wholly unnatural docility —a docility which probably helps account for matriarchal tendencies in certain marriages.

Another misplaced emphasis would certainly be the overwhelming preoccupation with the *virginity* of Mary. It is not our intention to question any dogma; we merely wonder if in glorifying the great Marian virtues we do not undermine much that we aim to strengthen. When we sing in the preface of Masses for feasts of the Blessed Mother "and losing not the glory of her virginity," do we not diminish the act which is extolled in every other marriage throughout history—the giving completely of man and woman to each other?

The Church speaks of the solemnity and the sacredness of the marriage act, and in its wisdom classifies as an impediment to marriage impotency and the withholding of the marital privilege. Hence, while the Church is directing the eyes of the faithful to the virginity of the Holy Family, it must paradoxically also stress the requirement of consummation. We do not find this ambivalence particularly difficult theologically, but it is disconcerting in practice. We think it contributes to a minimizing of that familial relationship, the giving completely of self, which is wholly as admirable (if not more so, because more natural and expressive of total love) as the combination of the virginal integrity of the Blessed Mother and the trustful resignation of St. Joseph. The paradox gave us pause. Our impulse was to ask ourselves whether our physical union as man and wife had any great place or merit apart from the procreation of children.

The raising of this question leads us to wonder whether the special preoccupation of the Church in America with virginity is not distorted. We wonder if the conscientiously chaste couple entering marriage is both unprepared for, uninstructed in, and unappreciative of the positive aspects of their physical relationship. The importance attached to the Sixth and Ninth commandments; the proliferation of sodalities of Our Lady, Dominic Savio and Maria Goretti clubs, to foster the virtue of chastity; the decency crusades against dirty books and busty movies; the campaigns for Marylike dresses—these and more give us serious doubts.

It does not, really, surprise us that marriage often is badly described by the very ones who should know better, the clergy and religious. In our experience, they speak of it as the state in which man and woman (a) release passion, (b) beget children, and (c) meet their obligations to society. How rare it is that we have heard of the growth in grace and sanctity which is possible through sexual union. This is something that we discovered for ourselves; we are astonished that it is not shouted from the pulpits. In many ways, a blissful sexual relationship is basic to all that is good and desirable in marriage. Husband and wife almost inevitably are better people, better parents, better citizens, better candidates for sainthood because they are better bedmates. But this is something that is not talked about. If the bedroom is mentioned from the pulpit, it is only to hammer at the sins against the laws on birth control that can be committed there. The approach is always negative. In our experience, the blessedly spiritual view of the bedroom is never glimpsed, or at least never mentioned.

Nevertheless, we are inclined to take an indulgent view of this "blindness" in the Church; after all, the bedroom is an exceptionally delicate topic, and the sexual relationship of husband and wife is so intimate that it confronts the preacher with challenges of tact, modesty, and inexperience which are unique to his situation. But at the same time, we cannot pardon it completely, for the silence on this subject is only the high point in a series of faulty emphases which stretch from the cradle to the grave. We were forced to discover for ourselves the spiritual possibilities of our physical association. Some couples, we dare say, never do, even though they might live happily, have children, and discharge adequately their responsibilities to God and society.

It was our good fortune to have made our discovery relatively early in marriage, yet it would not have been surprising had we not made it at all. For our background was one in which Sisters instructed us that sins against the Sixth Commandment were the most evil in the eyes of God. I recall a priest telling of a young boy who said in his first confession that he had committed adultery; for the lad was convinced that he had sinned in the worst way possible, and Sister had drilled into his seven-year-old mind that the worst sin was adultery; so to this he confessed, though all he had done was to urinate against a church building. We remember parish priests who blunted the masculine writings of St. Paul by avoiding the strong word "fornication," as in the epistle of the ninth Sunday after Pentecost, and using an embarrassed, general phrase, "gross immoralities." We also remember opposition to mixed male-female education, even under Catholic auspices, on grounds that undue familiarity between opposite sexes was likely to stir sinful curiosity. Under the circumstances, it is a blessing that inhibitions about sex, and feelings of guilt, were not carried into our marital bedroom. The fact that some Catholic married couples suffer in their sex lives from scrupulosity is not to us the least bit astonishing. The amazing thing is that many more do not.

But one cannot hold the Church and its religious totally to blame for the grim attitude toward sex in marriage which caused us and which causes others puzzlement. In our case, as surely in others, parents on both sides of the family bear a measure of responsibility. In each of our homes (which were in cities miles removed from each other) sex was never a remote, mysterious, marvelous interplay between mother and father. The illusion was created that sex did not exist at all. A chum once remarked to me that pregnancy must be an airborne disease. Further, the subject was never admitted into conversation; and there was no such thing as sex instruction or counsel. Even parental displays of affection toward each other were confined to a ritualistic, hurried peck of a kiss on leaving for or arriving from work. In other words, there was little joyous spontaneity, little to convey to us children that our parents, by the very fact of their co-habiting, were about God's business.

So it was, in any case, that my wife and I moved into marriage, unrealistically and incompletely readied for it psychologically by either home or Church. It would be pleasant to report that we immediately saw the fallacies of the system and adjusted our lives accordingly. But we did not. We recall now with an embarrassed hilarity the disapproval we felt toward the practice of a friend who, when pregnant, used to place the hands of her youngsters on her stomach to acquaint them with the new brother or sister who would soon be theirs. This was a wonderfully devout gesture, and one that was accompanied by an explanation of the spiritual and physical significance of the movement the children felt. But it shocked us, and we were married then a year or more.

Over the years we have attempted to establish in our home a more relaxed, more roundedly Christian atmosphere with regard to sex; we have sought to make our home one that is not dominated as were the homes of our youth by a morality that has little dimension or depth aside from the sexual. We have fostered modesty among our children, but with a care that this was not done at the expense of the dignity of sex. We have guarded against the shame and furtiveness which were part of our own experiences as youths. We have encouraged openness and frankness.

To a degree we have been successful. Our children come to us with questions my wife and I never dreamed of taking to our parents; they are comfortable in situations that would have made us blush deeply. But we have succeeded only so far— partly because of our own lingering inhibitions; partly because as the children grow older they come more under the influence of external forces, notably the parochial school. Thus our home code is abridged or supplanted.

We recently took the problem of our children's narrowing attitude toward sex to a clergyman whose sense of sexual morality is more Latin (and accordingly more healthy) than American. He sympathized, but could offer no great help. "The problem is in the air they breathe," he commented.

As much as we dislike it, as much as we struggle against it, my wife and I can see elements of our former moral anxiety accumulating bit by bit in our children, though they are all still in their pre-teens. Whatever their premarital behavior, if they are raised entirely in America they are almost certain to enter marriage with infusions of Puritanism from their worldly environment and of Jansenism from their religious training. This is a worry to us, for sex in marriage could then become for them less an expression of love than a form of self-gratification. If they are devout, there might also be the silly suspicion that, even though lawful, sex within marriage will intrude upon rather than assist communication between them and God. As my wife and I found out after we were married, quite the opposite is the case. We would like our children to be aware of the fact before they enter marriage.

The challenge, therefore, would seem to be in creating a

climate in which it is taken for granted that sanctity in marriage depends as much on the act of union as it does on the fruits of union; that within the morality of marriage itself there is nothing ignoble or embarrassing, ever, about marital romance. We would like to work for a Christianity in which the accent in marital relations is on the solemnity, not the mere lawfulness, of the couple's sexual union.

Our guess is that when a sharper perspective is gained on the sacredness of the body and sex in marriage, there will be considerably less difficulty about the secondary, more occasional problems of sex in marriage, which we have hardly touched on in our account.

CHAPTER ELEVEN

A Mixed Marriage

Mr. and Mrs. K have been married four years and have one child, a year old. Mr. K is an investment banker.

Mr. K writes first:

My wife and I are veterans of over four years of marriage. We are both close to thirty and have one child, born a year ago. My wife is a born Catholic, educated through the college level in Church institutions. I was raised a Presbyterian and remain outside the Church, although I find myself increasingly attracted to Catholicism.

Our marriage has been a source of joy, pleasure, and fulfillment as well as of anxiety and doubt. As in every marriage, the union of imperfect people, ours is sometimes beset by misunderstanding and the lack of communication. Through the act of sex, we attempt to reestablish the dedication to charity which is the foundation of our marriage vows. Within the conflicts of our relationship, we find satisfaction from the mutual understanding that we achieve from facing life together.

It has been our experience that love becomes richer through the facing and overcoming of the sexual doubts which we brought into our marriage. I was brought up to feel that sexual gratification was a mysterious pleasure reserved for marriage, like smoking and drinking. Sex was not mentioned in relation to love. When spoken of at all, which was rare, sex was mentioned either in a humorous or embarrassed vein. I received no formal sex education. My parents believed that one's natural instincts would somehow lead one to "do the right thing" when the time came. I cannot remember that sex was in any way discussed as a form of communication between lovers.

In the tradition of my middle-class Protestant background, moral issues were rather vaguely defined. I was taught to live by the principles mentioned in the Bible, as best as I could puzzle them out. In relation to my own situation, these applied to acts like stealing and cheating. Sexual morality was beyond my grasp. Of course, I knew that there were certain social taboos with regard to sex, but I was totally unaware of any moral issues involved. With my lack of sex education, I was left on my own with the assumption that natural instinct, disciplined by social mores, would enable me to act correctly.

As I reached adolescence, I found myself afraid of exploring physical relations with girls, because of my ignorance. I felt somehow that it was not nice, not polite. The impulses within me I thought were somehow selfish in nature, a biological necessity for the gratification of my own desires, but certainly not a source of mutual pleasure. The result of this attitude was that I approached marriage entirely ignorant of the role that sex plays. Sexuality as a moral issue was simply beyond me. It is not that I did not learn that premarital intercourse was morally wrong. It's that I was not taught that any form of sexual arousement before marriage was proper. In this vacuum, I was unable to distinguish morally between advanced sexual contacts and the more innocuous forms.

In our courtship, my wife and I began to explore the sensations of physical pleasure which we found that we could give each other. These explorations were modest, consisting primarily of the most elemental physical contact. The important point for us, however, was that the exploration was being done mutually. We were learning and enjoying together. Throughout the period of our courtship, we discovered that the sexual impulses were not divorced from the expression of love. There was something fundamental and satisfying in the physical pleasure which had begun to be so meaningful to us. I must add that this courtship was carried out within the bounds of Catholic doctrine. We went neither too fast nor too far, feeling bound by the strictures of my wife's faith.

This was another important early lesson that we learned. Sexual intimacy, for us, could only be fully pleasurable when it did not affront conscience. We did not feel that disobedience of the laws of the Church was a foundation upon which we wanted to build our marriage. We felt that when we were married we could explore more fully the pleasures of sex. The important thing for us, before marriage, was that we proceed slowly, not taking for granted the other's feelings or impulses. By teaching each other, we came to appreciate more fundamentally the responsibilities of our separate sex roles.

Following our marriage, our first attempts at intercourse were characterized more by patience than by passion. Each was ambitious that the other experience maximum pleasure from the act. We both knew that sex is not a toy, that intercourse is an act of responsibility and maturity before it is an act of pleasure. In the early days of our marriage, we tended to concentrate more on technique and timing than on sensation.

Intercourse, and the love play leading to it, were new experiences for us. What I was taught as a boy, that intercourse would come naturally, was wrong. Successful intercourse, in which both partners experience physical bliss, is an act requiring great skills in foreplay, timing, and attitude. For me, this did not come easily. As a man, I found the most important problem was to refrain from getting too excited too quickly. My wife's constitution was such that she required extensive foreplay and the patient conditioning of all her senses in preparation for climax. I learned very soon that by indulging my own sensations I was unable to gauge the intensity of her responses. Once having reached climax myself, I was almost totally unable to continue the activities which would bring her to the same state if she were not with me at the time.

This taught me consideration for the slower pace of my wife's stimulation. To give her pleasure, I had to learn to control my own progress. This regard for my wife, which she instinctively felt, has deepened our respect for each other. The result has been the achievement of simultaneous climax in our more experienced efforts which is a source of supreme pleasure to both of us.

I regard simultaneous climax as the most important achievement of sexual activity. It is an accomplishment that can only result from the submission of one's own desires to the needs of one's partner. This act of self-restraint nurtures the feeling of understanding which must develop in marriage. The concern that my wife would be unable to experience the most blissful sense of pleasure from intercourse is a primary consideration in my sexual activity. Morally, I think it would be wrong to consider intercourse strictly as the gratification of one's own desires. Marriage is the sharing of all pleasures and the fulfillment of the partner's desires as well as one's own. If this ambition is not fundamental in the sex act, there is a violation of the purpose of matrimony.

It is the nature of things that the male is quick to be aroused and just as quick to be satisfied. I know that following climax I very rapidly lose interest in further love-making. I am fatigued and want to do nothing but rest. On the other hand, my wife is slower to arouse and less quickly exhausted by climax. For her, climax is the midpoint in intercourse, which she wants to be followed by additional expression of love. Once again, I feel it would be morally wrong for the husband to follow his natural instincts. Immediate withdrawal would be a source of disappointment to the wife, destroying the tenderness of the moment. I think it is incumbent on the husband to continue offering the same endearments which are so meaningful to the wife's experience. Selfishness cannot be allowed to intrude on the intimacy of intercourse. I think that natural instincts, divorced from the discipline imposed by charity, are basically selfish. If I were to make love instinctively, I would very quickly reach a state of arousement, achieve climax, and withdraw exhaustedly. I can't believe that this would ultimately have any meaning for her or for me.

Marriage is the giving of oneself to one's partner. Like all human acts, this one too is far from being perfect or even completely satisfactory. It is the application of patience and practice which achieves the joy that marriage has to offer. Over four years, the act of intercourse has become less self-conscious and more spontaneous. The physical pleasure of sex has become more rewarding. As timidity and shyness are overcome by understanding, we find that intercourse has become much more fun, much less of a duty. It would be wrong to say that every performance of the sex act results in simultaneous climax and the maximum ecstatic sensations. Satisfaction varies from mediocre to excellent for a variety of reasons. At times, we tend to take sex for granted, to rush through the preliminaries and to disregard the fact that emotions must be carefully built up.

I think it is morally wrong to lose sight of the fundamental purposes of intercourse in a rush to achieve physical satisfaction. Since intercourse is the sharing of each other's joy, we try always to approach it with consideration and patience. It is the effort made in trying, and the realization that this effort is made in consideration of the partner, that helps us achieve mutual understanding. Each act, whether perfectly or imperfectly performed, gives us the experience to approach the next attempt with a surer concept of what is required of us. The fact that we are learning and growing together has given our marriage a more profound basis of understanding.

Love in a marriage is the charity which forgives the frailties that mar the union. Forgiveness, in turn, is the outgrowth of understanding and trust. By understanding, I mean that I seek to appreciate my wife's desires and needs and to fulfill them as best I can. By trust, I mean that I know that I cannot fully satisfy all her desires and that it is the sincerity of the effort, more than the perfection of the results, that cements our union. When simultaneous climax is not achieved, there is a sense of frustration and disappointment. It is imperative at this point that the greatest degree of charity be shown. Once again, it is not a question of natural instincts, but of the fulfillment of the Christian duties of the husband to the wife. He is bound to show her love and respect. Failure to do this at the critical moment of an ill-timed climax is a breach of his obligation.

Sexual contact is one of the many forms of communication in marriage. It is the most important and the most rewarding. The sex act implies intimacy, the achievement of which is the real goal of marital communication. When intimacy is established in marriage through the creation of understanding and trust, then it is continuously renewed through every other form of communication. Physical contact is the heart of intimacy. Through the sharing of this most personal pleasure, the fundamental desire of giving oneself is satisfied. Sexual intercourse gives me pleasure for two reasons. First, it is the source of delightful sensation to my wife. Second, and equally as important, it affords me the same joy. By sharing this experience, the physical is combined with a spiritual delight. My physical pleasure is intensified by the knowledge that I have been able to give my wife the same sensation. I think this is the heart of the marriage communion.

We have practiced rhythm from the beginning of our marriage. My wife is a Catholic and cannot in good conscience condone the use of contraceptives. Her mental reservations about birth prevention would prohibit her from enjoying sexual intercourse artificially terminated. Since her pleasure is the source of my own, any of her anxieties would communicate themselves to me and my own satisfaction would be lessened. We have never used contraceptives nor have we even had the temptation. From a psychological standpoint, the thought of contraceptives is repugnant to both of us. For her, her upbringing has conditioned her to the point that complete fulfillment would be impossible. For myself, her satisfaction from our simultaneous climax is so important to my own happiness that contraceptives are ruled out.

During my non-Catholic upbringing, the subject of contraceptives was not discussed. I learned about them in the locker room and was unaware of the moral issues. I have always thought of contraceptives as unnatural, although I had no spiritual guidance on this point until later in my life. My wife and I have never been tempted to consider artificial birth control because of our sense of responsibility regarding intercourse. The thought has never occurred to us that the act might be performed only for gratification and nothing else.

The practice of rhythm brings us closer together spiritually and physically. During the periods of fertility we share the abstinence from intercourse as a sacrifice we both wish to make. Mutual abstinence is easy for us to bear because we know it's for our own good. This is not to say that sexual pleasure is absent during this period. On the contrary, physical contact becomes even more pleasurable as an end in itself. It is not hurried through in the eagerness to perform more profound acts. We become more aware of the satisfactions of other forms of intimacy as ends in themselves. We are able to rekindle the pleasure of our courting days by delighting in more innocent forms of contact. These periods are important to us also because we become aware that sex is not the only means of communication in marriage. We share ourselves intellectually and appreciate more the social nature of the marriage union.

With the arrival of the nonfertile period, we are able to approach intercourse with reborn enthusiasm. We are introduced all over again to the pleasures of maximum satisfaction. The scarcity of time available for intercourse makes each opportunity more meaningful to us. A parallel would be a man alternating a diet of very rich, spicy food with plain fare. Abstinence from the rich food makes its consumption more pleasurable because there is no feeling of satiation.

At the same time, a pressure develops between us to make each experience one of maximum satisfaction. This creates a danger that we try to put too much emphasis on intercourse and too much importance on satisfaction. We sometimes lose perspective and feel that failure to achieve simultaneous climax is somehow a failure in communication. Perhaps if there were more opportunities for intercourse, we would not be so self-conscious. On the other hand, I think that abstinence forces us to approach intercourse more soberly, more conscious of the God-granted pleasure which marriage affords.

The sex act is the expression of physical and spiritual love of one human being for another, climaxed in one supremely pleasurable moment, but shared in memory forever between the partners. The fruit of the union is born in love, in the self-realization that comes from the successful meeting of the responsibilities of marriage. I believe that marriage, as every other responsibility in life, is a test of our ability to do our best to carry out God's will.

To put sex in perspective: it is our most beautiful memory. The flooding of sexual desires within me renews the appreciation of my wife's beauty. Intercourse is a source of joy because we are able to give each other pleasure. It is the supreme responsibility because it lies at the very center of our marriage. It is the intimacy through which understanding is achieved, and it is the creative act by which man participates in the Divine plan.

Mrs. K:

I have had a kind of anxiety about the use of sex because of our use of rhythm. I questioned the need for it. Being a

Catholic, I checked with my confessor and was reassured by him of the morality of its use. His advice was a source of reassurrance to me, because being married to a non-Catholic creates an added responsibility for me in that I carry the burden of the doctrinal purity of our marriage myself. I do not believe basically that ours is a "mixed" marriage. To me, our marriage is the achievement of mutual consent and understanding between the partners. My husband has pledged to respect the requirements of the Church before we were married. It is not his signature on a document that assures me he will do this, but my respect for him as a person seriously trying to do his duty as a Christian. Our marriage is built on respect and there is nothing "mixed" about our convictions that mutual respect is the keystone of our union.

I believe it is the duty of the wife to satisfy her husband's desires. In my education both at home and in the Catholic schools, I was taught that sex was a responsibility of married life. I had been taught to avoid sexual arousement as a single girl because I would be tempted to go too far. Any activities that could lead to sexual intercourse I was taught were wrong. The bounds of proper behavior of a Catholic girl were concretely drawn and I did not feel a desire to exceed them. My mother and my teachers instructed me in the proper role of a Catholic wife and in the restraint that was needed prior to marriage.

Suddenly after vows made in the sacrament of matrimony, my attitude was supposed to change magically. Sex became the duty of a married couple for the consummation of the marriage and the procreation of children. I found myself somewhat bewildered and not a little frightened. The barriers were down, there was no further need to practice restraint; on the contrary, to do so would be to violate the purpose of marriage. I did not know that sex should be an enjoyable experience. I was so self-conscious about making a mistake or of not being able to please my husband that I was uneasy about the whole experience. I was not taught that marriage was supposed to be fun, among other things.

I learned that sex should be enjoyed by both partners in order to achieve the spirit of love and happiness, which is the ideal of the sacrament. Only can the vocation of the marriage state be truly fulfilled with mutual understanding and love when there is a joyous giving of oneself to one's spouse. This is difficult to achieve when sex is done out of a sense of duty rather than with enjoyment. Moral anxiety can occur if there is any doubt in the wife's mind about depriving her husband of pleasure. It is wrong to feel that the wife must submit to what she thinks is her husband's pleasure. Sex is not submission, it is cooperation and this is what brings about mutual satisfaction.

If rhythm is used, it must be practiced by mutual consent. Consideration is essential. Because of abstinence over a period of time, I become aware of the stronger appetites of my husband and I respect him for the control of those appetites. We practice rhythm by mutual agreement. We wish to carefully raise and educate our children to their Catholic maturity and wish to devote our energies to a fewer number of children than we are physically capable of having. The understanding and consideration of the partners is essential when rhythm is practiced. Out of love for my husband and the enjoyment of the complete satisfactions of sex, we experience joy in intercourse whenever the opportunity is available.

We do not feel, because we practice rhythm, that we are depriving each other of pleasure. Enjoyment of sex is not marred in any way by abstinence. On the contrary, I believe we have come to respect each other to a greater degree because of the sincerity of the effort on both our parts to raise our family according to the program we both wish to follow. Abstinence is as important as intercourse in our marriage. The exercise of self-control is rewarding in the achievement of self and mutual respect. In our marriage, this is even more rewarding to me because the difference in our backgrounds could create misunderstanding in place of respect.

Consideration plays a great part in our lives, not just for the first year of our marriage, but continuously. We are aware of the differences in our sexual appetites, and the tailoring of our own activities to the needs of the spouse brings respect and a deeper feeling of love. It is important that the physical needs of the spouse be considered, but even more significant, in my opinion, are the moral needs. Mutual love goes deeper than physical satisfaction, and we have never tried to isolate sex from the other aspects of our marriage. Christ is the center of our marriage. It is important to me to bring my husband to an understanding of the Catholic faith through my own example. I believe this can best be achieved by patience, self-sacrifice, and respect for his beliefs.

CHAPTER TWELVE

Embracing
the Absurd

Mr. and Mrs. L have five children. Mr. L, who has written of their experience, is a professional man and a daily communicant as his wife was, "and will be once more, when the age of the children permit."

Mr. L writes:

What may be of special interest in my case is that I had the advantage of several years of seminary life. In the light of those years I would like to make the following comparison. The vow of chastity was for me, as it would be for most young men, a difficult undertaking, but I did not leave the seminary on that account. I found chastity, under seminary conditions, to be difficult but entirely possible. Rather it was the essential loneliness of the celibate life which I found impossible. The vocation of marriage, therefore, has been my path to God. But I would not say that it has been, in all respects, the "easier" vocation. It is precisely in the respect that as a seminarian I had thought it would be easier, that it has been harder; namely, sex. A paradox, perhaps, but one which is, after a moment's reflection, believable.

I am of such a temperament—and surely it is not an uncommon one—that I could practice complete sexual abnegation, given practical distance from the opposite sex. On the other hand, impulsive and spontaneous by nature, I find close proximity with the other sex a more-or-less overwhelming experience. There is no "practical distance" in marriage; yet there surely are many long periods when sexual abnegation is called for. This is why I say that with regard to sex, and abstracting from the larger problem of loneliness, married life has proved to be more difficult for me than seminary life.

Rhythm, of course, is the big problem. I would like the theologian to be aware of the facts here. For any vigorous man in his twenties or thirties, sex gets to be obsessive as weeks of restraint roll by. Nocturnal emissions may relieve desire in a manner unobjectional to the moralist, but hardly so to the psychologist. Or, to be very frank, if passion is not thus relieved, it may reach such an unhealthy intensity that sex relations, when they finally do begin, suffer from it. During "safe" periods, on the other hand, couples may begin to feel an "obligation" to have relations. Biological calculation begins to replace joy and affection. Now, I am a firm believer in natural law. Natural law is to me one of a precious handful of concepts that help to make sense out of the jungle of human relations today. Yet, speaking from experience, few things seem less "natural" to me about married life than rhythm—unless it be the use of mechanical contraceptive devices, which tempt me not in the least.

Then why practice rhythm? Are we sure we have no selfish motive, preferring our own ease and comfort perhaps to the additional toil, trouble, and expense of giving God more children? The reasons for using rhythm are quite clear for us—clearer since my wife had a minor breakdown. Professional theologians are not unaware of the difficulties of married people, but let our little story be told, because our virtues, weaknesses, and motivations are typical.

Our fifth child was born after seven and one-half years of marriage. My wife's health had broken down while she was carrying the fifth. So we decided to practice rhythm (still with an occasional scruple about lack of trust in God). But it so happened that year that my wife's period was delayed one month for almost two weeks. We were sure she had become pregnant. Toward the end of those weeks I came home from the office one day to find the house in disorder, my wife sitting distraught on the floor of the living room with the children gathered around her. She was immobile, unable to care for them. When I tried to encourage her to get up, and said that things would somehow work out all right, she broke down. For nearly thirty minutes, she could only repeat over and over again, "You don't understand, you don't understand."

There was no one in my family nor in her own who could help us. I was not in a financial position to hire any help. Was she thinking of her own ease and comfort when she broke down? Perhaps. She is a human being. But I know my wife. She is capable of great sacrifice; much more than I am. What primarily caused her breakdown was the thought that she could not continue to take care of the five children we already had - the eldest still only in the first grade. That was the worst day in our lives. How we prayed to be spared another child, for at least another year or two! And our prayers were answered. No doubt our trust in God was not exemplary. But let the clergy know—most of them do—that heroism is not the exclusive demand of the religious state.

And yet, at this point, I want to address my fellow laymen, returning to my dialogue with the theologians in a moment. I am as devoted a disciple of Teilhard, as enthusiastic an exponent of alert Christian humanism as anyone else. But when I think even of the best lay people I know today, I have a few misgivings. Let us agree, to begin with, that it is absurd to suppose we are not much affected by living in an age which, as Philip Wylie once put it, "is technically insane on the matter of sex." It is not that educated Catholics are using contraceptives; Catholic sociologists have found some evidence to indicate that better educated Catholics are more faithful to the mind of the Church on these things than are those with less education. This seems to reverse the old wive's tale about learning being dangerous to the faith. No, it is not that Catholics in intellectual circles break the rules; it is just that they are so bitter about them. My own tendencies in the matter are clear enough. I have only just finished talking about the "unnaturalness," indeed, the absurdity of rhythm. Oh, the bitterness I myself have both heard and felt on this subject!

Granted that we appreciate sex today, perfecting mystery that it is, on many more levels than did the medieval schoolmen. But has there not been, in our times, some tendency to genuflect before it? No matter how rich, how ennobling, how mysterious the marital act is, it is surely a flat lie, and a very suspicious one, to maintain that personal love cannot survive its interruption. The tensions, the absurdities, occasionally the agonies of practicing rhythm can do nothing to destroy the love of husband and wife, unless they have not, to begin with, some commonsense, rock-bottom Christian concept of what love is about. And in that case the only thing to be destroyed is some romantic illusion of love, which may be all to the good, if there is any possibility of personal growth. We ought not to find the cross of Christ a scandal.

The best advice I ever got on rhythm came to me from a cloistered monk who knew nothing about it and refused to presume to advise me. He talked instead about the life of a Christian. "Lay people do wrong," he said, "and so do their spiritual directors, to suppose when they pick up St. John of the Cross or some other mystical writer, that the so-called 'dark nights of the soul,' or 'dark nights of the senses' do not pertain to anyone not wearing a religious habit. Or even if they think it relevant for laymen, they find that the steps toward progress laid down by St. John or St. Teresa have no correspondence in their lives, so they put the book away. As if God works chapter by chapter! As if he operated by spiritual geometry! Something like a 'dark night of the soul' or 'dark night of the senses' is going to hit any Christian, layman or cleric, if he is striving for God. In one form or another, whether John of the Cross, writing several centuries ago, could accurately describe it or not, some kind of a 'dark night' is going to hit the modern layman too. There is no reaching after God except in the dark. What is more, I think the whole Church probably goes through 'dark nights'—times when she appears ridiculous—times following some scientific breakthrough, perhaps, when this or that dogma, or book of scripture, appears absurd, and it is not yet given to the Church to know how to answer. Then we cling in the dark to our faith. It's all we can do for a while, although we pray for light and work for light. Light always comes. As if to reward the Church for faith, Christ sends light. The absurdity disappears as if by magic. The answer is so simple we wonder how it was not immediately evident in the previous century. But we can be sure that further dark nights lie ahead."

I take rhythm to be the "dark night" of this half of the twentieth century. I have given up attempts to make my position intelligible to Protestants and Jews who question me on the matter. I tell them that it is a matter of conscience with me, and I do not presume to judge their conscience on the matter. I am content to appear a bit ridiculous. They do not break off their friendship; all humans are ridiculous in one way or another—this is *my* way. I have also given up trying to understand the ethics of rhythm myself. The Church has spoken. It is enough.

There are more scientists now alive than all the scientists of days gone by put together. It is practically a foregone conclusion that in the next ten to twenty years there will be some important biochemical breakthrough on the problem of fertility prediction—some simple skin test, perhaps, by which the exact day of fertility is revealed. It is highly unlikely that children today will ever have to suffer this particular tension in their marital lives. I thank God that my children will be spared this particular purgatory. At the same time I am quite certain that some other problem, some other absurdity, some other dark night lies ahead to confront them. Except that this future problem will be equally excruciating—that much is guaranteed —I do not know the nature of it.

Now I would like to return to the theologians and the hierarchy. If I have everything so nicely figured out, and if I have found solace for my soul, what do I want of them? Let me say first what I don't want.

About three years ago I heard a story that filled me with bitterness and disgust. It seems that one well-known American Catholic university was offered a large sum of money by a foundation to carry out research connected with the rhythm method of birth control—ovulation detection, and so on. And in the midst of all the suffering, physical, mental and spiritual, now going on in thousands, rather millions, of Catholic families because of this problem, this Catholic institution turned down the grant because the project was, listen to this, "controversial!" What spiritual cowardice, what hardness of heart! Wives and mothers of Catholic families are having nervous breakdowns, untold thousands of men and women are cut off from the sacraments—is it 30 per cent, or is it 60 per cent of the Catholic population of adults in their twenties and thirties?—and this university finds research on rhythm "controversial."

And this leads me to what it is I have to ask of our theologians. I, for one, have always agreed with St. Thomas that theology is the queen of the sciences. Neither modern medicine nor nuclear physics have replaced her, in my estimation (although she ought not to disdain the contributions of either

one). Millions of loyal Catholics look to our theologians for
counsel on crucial issues—and not only marital problems, but
all the apocalyptic, scary crises of modern times, including
nuclear warfare. In the midst of all this psychological and
spiritual confusion I have to ask the theologians, "Are you, too,
afraid of being 'controversial'?" What a responsibility before
God is yours—in some ways as great as the responsibilities of
bishops, since it is you, frequently, who form their consciences
as well as ours.

When we laymen talk about these matters, the scarcity of
theological directives is always remarked upon. Theology is, for
us, an awesome science. Are the practitioners equally awesome?
Does anyone risk a minority opinion? Does anyone risk reputation as the price for doing a service to Mother Church? We
understand that even St. Thomas Aquinas was once an object
of suspicion to the Inquisition. Fortunately for the Church,
Thomas sought truth, rather than safety. I have already made
it clear that I am not a hero; do I demand heroism of you? I
suppose the answer is yes.

It is quite true that the cross is always with us, and that when
the problem of rhythm is solved, some equally agonizing problem will present itself. But I would hate to see theologians
turning that rather steely bit of consolation into a premise for
quietism. It has ever been the Christian dynamic to recognize
that our own brains are part of God's Providence. He *expects*
us to control cancer, as He expects us to control hunger. If
not today, tomorrow; it is a sin to give up the human attempt.
Population and birth have now entered the area of human responsibility. This gives the same glory to God, I should think,
as man's triumph over the haphazard "irresponsible" occurrence
of floods.

I have wondered whether under certain conditions it might
not even be sinful for two people to bring children into the
world. For to say God wants babies is only half the story; He
wants Christians. And it is not hard for me to conceive of

parents who, given their finite resources (psychological even more than financial), have to choose between giving God four Christians or eight delinquents. This is no laughing matter. It was when my wife was ill and carrying her fifth child that one of our other children, denied his usual quota of parental attention, began to masturbate. It has not been an easy matter to curb him of the habit. What would those writers of Catholic family manuals, who so indiscriminately praise large families, have to say about my little boy's falling into the habit of masturbation because of inadequate attention?

It appears then that the birth of more children can, in some circumstances, work to the *spiritual* hardship of the other children. When this is the case, when children already born are not put firmly on the path of salvation because of the general chaotic conditions and inadequate attention occasioned by still more births, I would question the responsibility of the parents. Or if they *are* responsible, and know what they are doing, I question their charity. Cannot one sin by *having* a child? We need norms and guidelines against exaggerations on both sides.

I don't wish to write as if I knew the answer to these questions. But these are the kind of questions I'd like to hear theologians discussing. And if they are presently still discussing the advancement of Our Lady's prerogatives, I am sure she would much rather have them get busy on the real needs of her people—the married here, and the poor around the world.

You who follow in the footsteps of St. Augustine and St. Thomas Aquinas, do manfully. Expose yourselves a little, and your reputations, if good for the Church will come out of it. Those of us who love Mother Church and who are loyal to her give you the last word. But you must speak it.

CHAPTER THIRTEEN

The Whole Scene

Mr. and Mrs. M live on the West Coast. They have five children.

Mr. M writes:

My wife was at the kitchen sink when I walked through the room; she had a knife in her hand and was chopping away at a bunch of carrots and thumbs. Or maybe it was celery and thumbs, anyway she was due to draw blood. Such sudden glimpses— she standing at the sink, intent, absorbed, the light streaming through the window over the sink, reflected and refracted by the water in the turtle tank on the windowsill— drive me wild. The water in the turtle tank needed changing and at any moment she was going to cut herself. I am brought to an awful awareness of her fragility and mortality. The woman I love is going to die; things can not hold: we are caught in a bewildering sea of awful change and relentless decay. Death too was reflected in the greenish waters of the turtle tank. "And nothing 'gainst Time's scythe can make defence, Save breed to brave him when he takes thee hence," Shakespeare said. I thought it, but I didn't say it. I didn't say anything, I did kiss the back of her neck.

"Have you looked at the calendar lately?" she asked, not looking up—luckily, of course, because the knife was still nicking away as busy as the scythe of Time.

I looked at the calendar, the same we had picked up at church last December. The calendar used to come to us through the courtesy of the local undertakers (24-hour telephone service), but now it advertises a grocery store. Not good thinking on the grocer's part: are we fattening ourselves but for the worms? The first thing my wife did last December was to tear off the penny-dreadful, air-brush pictures of the saint of the month, then with Scotch Tape and thumbtack she affixed the calendar to the wall of the kitchen. About that calendar our lives would revolve for a year. It shows at a glance the day of the week, the Saint of the day, and the progress of the menstrual cycle. Through this calendar we attempt to impose a pattern of some kind on the bewildering sea. One way or another the attempt is fruitless.

Pregnancies are tricks played on Time. And there is such joy during my wife's pregnancies, oh, such manifold joys. First, it is best when only she and I share the secret—and of course the doctor who has confirmed it. ("Oh, yes; big as an orange.") But he doesn't count and the world doesn't count, and it is our secret, our trick, our gift to the world at large. But then it is even more joyful when the whole world knows; a joy that allows us to rise above the snide remarks of those couples who have fewer children and the smug smiles of those who have more. ("Well, it's a competitive society, but maybe He'll change that too.")

But the best thing of all is the change in our relationship to the calendar. No more need we wrestle with Time, no more need we try to impose a pattern on Time—nor do we feel that we are submitting to Time. We are taking part in Creation itself. The days of the week are unimportant. ("Oh, guy, look what we missed last week!" "So call 'em up and tell them we're pregnant.") The time of the month is of no consequence; only the Saint of the day is important. Ferial days send us grumpily from the calendar to the *Concise Biographical Dictionary of the Saints*: "John the Dwarf, *Fifth Century*, he was remarkable for his simplicity and absent-mindedness."

("I know it's wrong of me but I can't abide the name John." . . . "Still, simplicity is a great virtue; particularly now." . . . "I don't want any more absentmindedness around this house. Who's tomorrow?")

And I, sitting at my typewriter, no longer rise to wander into the kitchen to check the calendar to see if it's worthwhile starting anything tonight. But then Time exacts payment. There is always the frightening night of labor: the baby is coming, will come, is coming *now*. Then there is no relief, no change of mind, no hesitation, no delay, no reprieve, no breathing spell. A few short months before we had made Time obey us. ("He moved; he really did. Here, put your hand here. Did you feel that?" And a life, almost as command, fluttered beneath my hand.) Now life and Time and everything else combine to overwhelm us, to frighten us, to remind us that we are always in the grip of inexorable change and in the shadow of death. And it is at that terrible moment when we need each other most that the doctor who hadn't counted says, "You'd better leave now." The father's room is three flights down.

"You can't *time* happiness," my wife just said. "If you try to time happiness you destroy it. Time is destructive of happiness; that's why there's no *time* in heaven. I think hell is probably just the marking off of every minute, you know, like in the dentist's waiting-room. Wouldn't that be hell?"

"Yes, but are you talking about sexuality in marriage?"

"I am. For instance, take the turtle tank."

"Turtle tank?"

"Yes, sure. I don't change the water when it's time; I change the water when it's green. And that turtle and that turtle tank give me great happiness when I stand at the sink washing the dishes every morning. He reminds me that there is a harmony to life, a pattern of change and recurrence that isn't the same thing as time at all.

"The funny thing is that we have discovered this about child-raising and we haven't discovered it about marriage itself, or about sexuality in marriage. When I stand at the sink washing the morning dishes and watching the turtle turn green, I know that along about eleven-thirty the baby is going to wake up and want his bottle. Now, a generation ago I would have been watching the clock so that I could poke the baby awake at eleven-thirty and feed him on schedule. It was the wrong way to treat a baby and it's the wrong way to treat a marriage."

"Well, yes, the poor baby," I said.

"And the poor marriage, when sex gets poked awake on schedule. Truly, my whole work schedule is affected. I mean, my happiness in the day is really dependent upon this: we might go to bed together tonight, if the kids are quiet and we feel like it, or not. No matter what I do during the day, the flavor is somehow gone when I know that we *won't*."

"*Won't*; but what about when we can't?"

"Well, that's natural. That's what I mean by harmony. Sometimes the menstrual cycle involves us, sometimes you're called away, but that's natural in marriage. It's not the same as *timing* ourselves."

"You're talking about rhythm, aren't you?"

"Sure; I'm saying that happiness doesn't lie that way. It isn't only *won't*; it's *will* too. Do you know what it's like working around the house all day knowing that we *will* tonight? We *will* tonight because we won't for the next two weeks. That knowledge doesn't only affect us at night, in the act, you know; it ruins my whole day."

"But sometimes . . ."

"Oh, sure, I know; but let's not kid ourselves into thinking that this is the way to get at happiness; we're just trying to pull through with a temporary, unhappy expedient."

I weigh my own memory of diurnal experiences against her

revelations of life at home, and I can only agree about the unhappiness of timing. But I add that what is the happy letting go, the carefree abandonment to nature's way that is woman's is not exactly the same as man's. The menstrual cycle still eludes me. There is a time when she is carefree, a time when she is moody, always that day when she doesn't want to be touched, and finally a time of relaxation and cheer. Such times are natural to woman, and natural to marriage, but not natural to man, who is a part of marriage. Even in the most carefree, natural sexual relationship in marriage there is a rhythm not *natural* to man. But is there a rhythm to me that I am unaware of, that my wife must come to terms with? I will ask her.

I address myself simultaneously to my typewriter and to my wife as I propose the question: What is the role of sexuality in our marriage?

"Well, it's the whole scene, the whole bit," she says. "If it weren't for sex, you and I would only be great chums." She uses slang like that only to cloak the body of a naked truth. Sometimes I must pierce the cloak, sometimes she will unbutton it for me. I wait, my fingers poised over the keys.

"I mean, why do you think I married you?"

I don't bristle easily, but I bristle well so she hurries on to soothe me.

"I don't mean it *that* way. When we were dating we weren't planning to go to bed or anything like, but I waited for you with such excitement because you were a man. I didn't feel that way when I had dinner with the girls. You were a man and you were a mystery. You still are."

"Sometimes I think you can read me like a book."

"Not really. That's just your naïve reaction to woman's intuition."

"Yeah? Well, what *is* intuition?"

"It's like speed reading, only of character."

"Is it fun?"

"Well, you can't just do it; it just is. See, you are asking questions that a woman would never ask. You know, I couldn't bear to spend my life with just women. Sex is really the basis of marriage; sex isn't only bed. It's the excitement and mystery of living with someone *not* like yourself. Everything you do, everything you are, is manly—even the way you try to be quiet, you know, thundering up the stairs on tiptoes when the kids are asleep. You're manly; I'm womanly and that's something quite different."

"You shave just as I do; you shave your legs."

"The very point. Do you?"

"You know I don't."

"Hey, that would be funny."

"Please, dear, this is an important subject: sexuality in marriage."

"I'm sorry."

"That's all right."

"You could use my Princess razor?"

"STOP."

"All right, I'm sorry. But, honestly, you men are so pompous when it comes to sexuality in marriage."

"This is a very important subject. The whole problem has been dominated by cleric-philosophers."

"I *said* I was sorry."

"*That* isn't your fault."

And she kissed me on the forehead and patted the typewriter and left the room to bed the kids down for the night.

What should I do? Should I run after her to tell her that she doesn't have a Princess razor? Should I tell her of my deep suspicion that she uses my razor to shave her legs. Should I simply follow her to tell her I love her—or had I better veer toward the kitchen and that calendar before I follow her?

The thing about marriage that clerics don't grasp is the sexuality that underlies the least action between husband and wife. The thing they don't know is that sex is the whole scene. (Where did I hear that before?)

When we all pile into the VW station wagon for church on Sunday morning and I hold the door open for my wife, or I don't hold the door open because I am wrestling the middle children into their safety belts, that is an action directly related to sexuality in marriage. I have instinctively reacted to her as woman, or I have not. And when we finally arrive at church and straggle into a rear pew ("Women and Children Only," says the sign, ordered up I suppose by a former pastor), that action too has sexual implications. And if one of the kids has a cold and sniffles all through Mass, that too will affect us sexually. One of us will be up during the night with nose spray and cough medicine. We don't really expect a sermon from the pulpit that will be a commentary on our unique, personal, mysterious relationship that has produced these kids.

Nor do we expect to find a commentary on our marriage in the Doctor books, or in the treatises written by Catholic sociologists. And the novelists! What is it with them?

"I do not believe," said my wife, "that *any* marriage has been made happier through the study of sexual organs."

"Oh, really?"

"Are doctors particularly happy in their marriages?"

"I'm sure I don't know."

"I don't know either, but I doubt it. Every time I get out the medical book to see what kind of a rash the kids are developing, the book opens to the diagram of *organs*. Is it true that they study these things in Pre-Cana Conferences?"

"Lord, I know less about them than I do about doctors."

"For instance, can you imagine sitting down to a lovely gourmet dinner . . ."

"Now, really, dear . . ."

"Yes, and thinking how you intend to masticate, or what hydrocarbonates are contained in what."

Again she has struck to the heart of the matter. "It's the feeling of a body for another body; it isn't the application of a principle." The doctrine of the Church is clear although sometimes warily applied. The sacrament of marriage is not conferred by the priest; it is conferred upon each other by the bride and groom. And the priest-clerics in a number of bold treatises have allowed that the sacrament is conferred ultimately by consummation. What all this seems to mean is that there is a mystery, a uniqueness, a not to be spelled-out condition to each particular sacrament of marriage. If orgasm, or a certain juxtaposition of organs, or a certain ecstasy were truly a part of marriage one would think that this would have been by now incorporated into the sacramental order. It isn't, of course; and without calling for a return to Victorian ignorance, my wife is pointing to the obnoxious intrusion of pseudoscience, klieg light illumination, and statistical computation into an area that must remain a mystery: the feeling of one particular body for another body.

Of course, doubts come to us sometimes, smoking together late at night: maybe we're the odd ones. Perhaps we should ask, what is it with us, not what's with the official commentators on sex in marriage. But there is a corporate strength in our marriage, and we assure each other that there is nothing wrong with *us*. "We're not the type, that's all."

"That's right, not the fine young athletes," I say.

"That's right."

"I think they just make all that stuff up."

There is no reply from her.

Well, what type are we then? I think this essay has illustrated to a certain extent what type, or at least what kind of marriage we have. We have an intellectualized, finely articulated, endlessly verbalized relationship that causes heart-scalding anguish when we are at odds; but brings too a heart-swelling awareness of love when we are as one. It all depends on how well we know each other at the moment, on how well attuned we are. The first years of our marriage, before the kids came and all, we followed each other about saying, "What are you thinking now?" We misinterpreted gestures and mistook answers

and sought explanations. It is the Fifth Commandment that
bears most directly on the marriage relationship, I sometimes
think. Now, we are skilled in interpretation and we have twelve
years of shared experiences, but the quest for knowledge about
each other is endless and endlessly rewarding. She is a mystery
because she is a woman. But I share that mystery through the
kitchen calendar, learning the cycle of the lunar month from
excitement through tension to depression. If the cycle is not
natural to me, at least the knowledge of the cycle is. We
can see the world at large through each other's eyes too, and
there still is room for mystery and surprise. For always she
knows more than I can know about her. Why in the world
didn't she say something when I suggested that novelists make
all that stuff up? What does she know?

There are sexual difficulties in such a marriage of course.
For one thing, our articulation doesn't extend to the area of
sex: our early training was too good for that. There are things
that we can't *say*, and even if we came to the point of saying
them the words would be largely meaningless because those
words lie so far removed from our ordinary vocabulary of words
supercharged with meanings through these dozen years of
shared experience.

For instance, when we find ourselves moody and despressed,
at outs with each other for heaven knows what cause, I react
to this condition out of all proportion to its real importance.
What apparently any Frenchman knows, and what every
novelist knows is that this irritability, this depression can be
dispelled by a quick tumble in the bed. Oh, it happens even
in the better biographies. But not around here. The professional commentators on sex have solved the problem, as I remember. There are cute devices that signal lascivious intent;
pink pillow cases, dimmed lights, even veiled looks. Awful
things and a lot of good they would do with the two of us
sunk in opposite chairs, pretending to read and neurotically
brooding on why and how the world has lost its savor.

And this restless attempt to know each other, to comprehend the loved one, which I have attributed to sex, gets in the way of what is usually referred to as sex. The fine old Elizabethan-Jacobean vocabulary denominated it as carnal knowledge, and the phrase is not without relevance. There is tactile knowledge of sorts, of course, which we shed along with pajamas, shyness and defenses. But this is a different kind of knowledge and in some ways not so rewarding as another kind. When even intense excitation can not drive out the awareness of Time's scythe, and the awareness of the otherness of the beloved; then we end more separate than before.

But of course we can brave old Time, and we have. And we have five kids to assure us of some kind of earthly continuance. "Nothing 'gainst Time's scythe can make defence, Save breed," Shakespeare said, and my wife said, "Sex makes beautiful babies." I had just consulted her for another valuable insight into the problem of sexuality in marriage. She was rocking the youngest, giving him his night bottle. There is no denying that his head is shaped like mine. But his head is shaped just like that of our eldest too, and she is one of our two adopted kids. I can offer no conclusions to this observation except to say that sex is still a mystery, despite the advancement of science.

After three years or so of marriage, and still childless, we submitted to a battery of fertility tests. There was only one acrimonious debate with a doctor about a sperm-count test. But one would think that the tests, taken all in all, would have driven the magic and mystery away. They didn't. But then began the regime of the kitchen calendar, supplemented by daily temperature recordings and carefully plotted or sometimes hastily arranged trysts. Nothing. Oh, well, the experience did bring us closer together in a rather children-against-the-storm pose. During the fourth year of marriage we completed a solemn triduum of Masses to Saint Anne on her feast day, asking for children. That day we received from a quite unexpected source the first word that we could immediately adopt our daughter, and that day, as subsequent events proved, we waxed pregnant. We were plunged headlong and nearly instantly ("Oh, three-day pregnancies are the worst.") into a maelstrom of children whose activities, whose demands, whose very presence has pretty well controlled our sexuality in marriage since.

"I wouldn't recommend any couple to do what we did," my wife said.

"What's that?"

"To try so hard for children."

"You think we did wrong?"

"No, no. But it wasn't a happy time for us."

"No."

"And you did look so chilly."

"Me?"

"Well, padding around barefooted in the morning, shaking down the thermometer, squinting at it in the dim light of dawn."

"I think I thought of myself as somehow, you know, noble."

"Well, that too. It didn't, as a matter of fact, get us children."

"No."

"I think prayer did, and the abandonment of ourselves to . . . well, I don't know to what; but we begot children when we least thought about it."

Sometimes she doesn't cloak the truth at all, she puts it clearly before me. We should not calculate how to impose the pattern of Time on our marriage, we should use our marriage to impose on Time, to defeat old Time. If Time is the enemy of happiness, and I accept her word for this, then we can use our marriage to defeat Time, for marriage makes us a part of the passing of generations. Only through marriage can we triumph over Time.

There are other ways to defeat Time. The priest is ordained into the order of Melchizedek, and the religious, nun or brother, can follow a way of life established centuries ago. There is nothing incongruous about a religious wearing a seventeenth century habit or a thirteenth century habit; but can you imagine a married person wearing such a rig? The sacrament of marriage catches us up in time and allows us to triumph over Time. Each marriage is unique and timed—the opposite of timeless, it is timed but triumphant over Time.

Suddenly it occurs to me why there is no marriage in heaven. Marriage is the sacrament of Time and Mystery, in heaven there is neither mystery nor time. I want to tell my wife to what new knowledge she has led me.

But she has gone to bed. She has tucked the babies in, praying over each, "Bless this child tonight and every night." Her very nearness and absence remind me of tomorrow. I will tell her tomorrow, although it will be different then. Again I am brought to the realization that I cannot know the universe or the secrets of the universe, I can know only her, and know her only day by day and night by night. Through the mystery of her I can faintly divine the mysteries of the world. Thank heavens for tomorrow.

This process of knowing the beloved one is at once continuous and organic. I see my wife anew each day in her relation to the children. I *know* her in the children in a new and startling way. And I know myself better too, for I see myself in the harsh light of their bright eyes and in the wondering look she gives me as I wax daily into a fury with one or another of the children. And oh, they have all taught me to love; even as I have scolded the children and punished them, they have taught me to love. It is the Fifth Commandment, not the Sixth or Ninth, that engages me: to what extent does charity tolerate anger?

So to sex . . . sexuality in marriage cannot, it seems to me at this point, be separated from the mystery that surrounds it. ("You men are so pompous . . ." "Yes, but even the outward sign of this sacrament is cloaked in secrecy and mystery." "I should hope.") To write, for instance, of periodic continence

or self-control or whatnot is irrelevant to the situation in which the only apparent manifestations are moodiness, a neurotic tendency to pretend to read a book, a willful closing of the mind. To write of sex without reference to the mysteries of grace so startlingly apparent in our own family, for instance, is foolish. To try to isolate sexuality in marriage is even more foolish because sex is the whole scene, as someone once said.